S0-AGM-738

Growing Up ADVENTIST

A fond look back at the church that taught me
faith, love, and laughter

ANDY NASH

Pacific Press Publishing Association
Nampa, Idaho
Oshawa, Ontario, Canada

Edited by Jerry D. Thomas
Cover illustration by Lars Justinen
Cover and inside design by Michelle C. Petz

Copyright ©1997 by
Pacific Press Publishing Association
Printed in the United States
All Rights Reserved

Nash, Andy, 1971-
    Growing up Adventist : a fond look back at the church that
taught me faith, love, and laughter / Andy Nash.
        p.   cm.
    ISBN 0-8163-1365-2 (paper : alk. paper)
    1. Seventh-day Adventists—Doctrines.   2. Seventh-day
Adventists—History. I. Title.
    BX6154.N365   1997
    286.7'32—dc21   96-50202
                                                      CIP

97 98 99 00 01 • 5 4 3 2 1

Contents

To Cindy:
I wish you had grown up where I did—
so I could have adored you sooner.

Preface

This book can be credited to one thing—an unfair article deadline imposed upon me the summer of '93 at the *Adventist Review*.

The villain in this case was associate editor, Roy Adams. Late one Thursday afternoon in June, Roy was editing an AnchorPoints article about the role of the church when he realized that he had room for a sidebar. Normally, Roy would have simply written the sidebar himself. But, as it happened, this particular week he was being shadowed by the kid, a summer intern from Southern College. *Why not?* figured Roy. And he passed the assignment onto me.

"What should I write about?" I asked Roy.

"Anything you like," he said, "as long as it has something to do with the church."

"How long do I have?" I asked, thinking *days*, maybe *weeks*.

"About twenty minutes," said Roy, laughing. "See what

you can do."

I did. I saw what I could do. And all I could do was write directly from my heart. No research. No interviews. No sleeping on it. *No time.* All I could do was take the word "church" and write the first words that came.

The words came from up north, from a modest little church in Detroit Lakes, Minnesota, where I grew up. "What makes a church special?" I asked my *Review* readers. Then I answered my own question by reminiscing about my old home church: the mornings of Bible stories and singing, the fun Christian friends, and the time I thought that the congregation was singing about me. "Andy walks with me," they sang, "Andy talks with me. Andy tells me I am his own." (For a while, I felt very honored.)

"A church's specialness," I asserted, "is not in the building. Rather, it's in the people and experiences inside." That was it. My twenty minutes were up, and I handed my article to Roy. He nodded, smiled, and said it would work fine.

Before the summer ended, I would get a couple more article assignments. In mid-July, I spent two full days on the phone, interviewing Adventist flood victims up and down the Missouri and Mississippi rivers. Then I spent several hours hammering out my story: "Waterlogged: Adventists Face the Flood of '93." It ran on the cover—a big deal, for a journalism student seldom published outside his college paper.

With a news story under my belt, I turned to feature

writing. Assistant editor Kit Watts asked whether I'd like to interview an Adventist astronomer who had been awarded an hour with the Hubble Telescope. I jumped at the chance. Two drives to Baltimore and a few long nights later, I excitedly turned in my story—"Ray Sterner: Studying the Moon, the Stars, and the Son"—and photos. The package was published, and I was flying high.

The peculiar thing, though, about the articles I wrote for the *Review* that summer was that I only got feedback to one of them—the sidebar about my little church in Minnesota. Hours and hours I had toiled at my other articles, crafting each sentence ("As the flood of '93 rises, crests, lingers, crests again, and finally recedes, Adventist families . . ."), blending powerful quotes ("Never in my life did I think I would cry to see it raining"), and shocking the world with my bold conclusions ("Only a Christian astronomer would dare say such a thing"). My Pulitzer acceptance speech was all but written.

Yet, no one seemed to notice those pieces. Instead, the only article to which people responded was the one that had meekly asked, "What makes a church special?"

"Nice piece about the church," said a man in the General Conference cafeteria.

"Your article about your childhood was so refreshing," a secretary told me.

"I really enjoyed your story about your little church in Minnesota," said a stranger several months later at Southern College.

"Andy walks with me, Andy talks with me," sang my obnoxious friends.

No one said a thing about my other articles—except Mom, who said she loved them all equally—and I wondered what the deal was.

Then, finally, it dawned on me. It wasn't that these people thought that my story about growing up Adventist was more important than a story about Adventist flood victims losing their homes or an Adventist astronomer working with the Hubble Telescope. Rather, they were responding to my sidebar because they could identify with it. Because it was close to home.

With that in mind, I called an old friend, *Review* editor William Johnsson, in January 1995 to see if he would be interested in a series about growing up Adventist. He said to send some samples. I did, the *Review* staff gave a thumbs-up, and the first installment, "Assigned Seating," ran in March.

In the months that followed, a few readers questioned the merits of such a series. "What place does 'Sabbath Afternoon Drives' have in the *Review*?" one man wrote. "Is Andy Nash trying to tell us how to keep our Sabbaths?"

"I couldn't care less about someone who went to a box social," wrote another.

"What was the point of 'Persecuted'?" another asked me directly.

I felt bad about these reactions. I didn't want my series to confuse anyone. And I knew that no writer should have to explain "the point" of an article. An article should stand alone.

Fortunately, most readers seemed to catch on. This series wasn't about theology, doctrine, or even Adventist her-itage. It wasn't about subtle symbolism, forcing a point, or working Jesus into every article. (As much as I wish that Jesus was the center of *every* aspect of my child-hood, it would be unfair—and, I think, unrealistic—to write as though He was.) It was just about life—the life of a typical Adventist kid. And that's why most people seemed to like it: By reading about my experiences, they were reminded of their own. "I always read your stories to my children," a woman told me. "Then I tell them my stories. They love it."

Along the way, the series even brought an unexpected twist or two. Apparently, one of my real-life characters, Virgil Krogstad, has become something of a folk hero in the Mid-west. Virgil recently told me how, one Sabbath, a farmer visiting from another town asked if he could take Virgil's picture. It seems that the farmer had had a little bet with his buddies regarding what Virgil looked like. (No word on who won the bet.)

This past December, the "Growing Up Adventist" series in the *Review* ended. It had to—the well was running dry. But before it did, I earmarked about 80 pages of new ma-terial for this book. Here, then, is a final look at growing up Adventist in one small American town in the early 1970s. Thanks for reading.

Thanks also to Roy Adams for giving me a lousy twenty

minutes to write my first *Review* article. If he had given me more than that, I probably would have written something dull.

Friday

The Detroit Lakes Seventh-day Adventist Church sits humbly on a small slope a mile north of town.[1] 404 Richwood Road is the address, but you don't need to know that unless you're mailing us something—a catalog of hot new ABC releases, perhaps. Just turn north at the Boys' Club, go down a little ways, and you're there. You can park either up by the sanctuary or down by the fellowship hall. If you've brought something for potluck, you'll probably want to park down below.

---

1. Detroit Lakes (pop. 7106), Minnesota, checks in halfway up the state on the far west side, a good three and a half hour drive from the Metrodome. Actually, it used to be called Detroit, Minnesota, but due to postal complications with Detroit, Michigan—people would write "Detroit, MN" on the envelopes they intended to send to the motor state, and our postman had fits trying to find 76th street—the city council added the word "Lakes." A wise decision, for each summer since, thousands of tourists, most of them from Fargo, flock to the town where they are sure to find lakes. "What are you doing this weekend, bud?" "Hey, we're going up to Detroit Lakes. Wanna come?" "Detroit Lakes? Sounds good; I'll come too."

You shouldn't have any trouble finding a spot. We have plenty of parking space at our church, and anytime it snows, which it does a lot, I ride along with Dad in our brown Jeep to plow it out. Dad says that when I get my driver's license, I can have my own snowplow route and make lots of money. Dad doesn't plow for money though. He wouldn't accept anyone's money even if they tried to pay him. I know this because I've watched people try to give him money.

"Here, Chuck, take this for your trouble."

"No, you keep it."

And as I stand there watching $10 and $20 bills being waved around carelessly, I can't figure out why Dad won't just accept the money. I would—I'd be happy to accept the money. There are a few things I'd like to buy.

On this day, a Friday in mid-November, Dad and I have spent the past twenty minutes pulling back the drifts from the downstairs entrance into a sizable mound. There's still quite a bit more to get, more than usual for this time of year, and they're predicting another six inches tonight, but we're hardly alarmed. We've learned by now that winter arrives here whenever it pleases. Winter likes Minnesotans and can't wait to spend some quality time with us.

"How many more days?" say the forming snowflakes to the cold wind.

"Oh, it won't be long now," answers the wind.

Winter doesn't schedule itself around such things as shopping trips to the cities or the seventh-day Sabbath, and while you must acknowledge its arrival, you don't let it change your whole lives. Which means you don't cancel church. It simply isn't an option.[2]

I can't remember ever missing church because of weather—though we're often late because of clothes. Mom and my sister Angel don't exactly see eye to eye on what's appropriate Sabbath attire. "You're not wearing those old clogs, are you?" I hear from upstairs as Dad and I sit in the living room and wait. I have to admit—we men have it pretty easy; we just grab the first suit and ironed shirt we can find.

The only slowdown is tying my tie. It usually takes me three or four attempts to get the back part just a little shorter than the front. Sometimes Dad has to help me. Finally, Mom and Angel come downstairs. Angel is smiling, but Mom is carrying a second outfit, complete with heels. The dilemma is far from settled—what Angel's wearing now might not be what she's wearing when she gets to church.

Once, we almost didn't make it to church at all. We were crossing one of the bridges that "ices quickly in winter" and

---

2. School, which relies on school buses, is a little more flexible. Several times each winter, Mom wakes me up with the five sweetest words in the English language: "School might be canceled today." Normally, it takes Mom three or four tries—each one increasing in intensity—to get me up, but on these days I spring out of bed and rush to the radio, hoping against hope. KDLM is going through the list of area schools: ". . . Audobon schools are running two hours late . . . Lake Park schools, canceled . . . Perham schools, two hours late . . . Frazee schools, canceled . . . Detroit Lakes schools, *on time*" (emphasis mine). I can't believe it: Detroit Lakes *always* has to one-up the other towns. As I search for my bath towel, I imagine some superintendent rolling over in his warm bed, picking up the phone, dialing KDLM, and saying, "Yeah, let's run Detroit Lakes schools on time today," as he flips his pillow to the cool side and falls back into a deep sleep.

sure enough, it had. We started sliding left. Dad frantically twisted the steering wheel hand over hand, but the black ice had us at its mercy. We slid across the center line and ricocheted off the opposite guard rail. No cars were coming. Then we spun back to the right guard rail and rattled against it until finally the tires regained traction. Dad downshifted and realigned the car; Angel realigned her clogs. No one said a word.

By the time I walked into Sabbath school, I wanted to say many words. I wanted everyone to know how close to death I had just been. How could they just sit there singing "Do Lord" when I had nearly been killed? I couldn't quite find the words to convey the trauma I'd been through,[3] so I just sat there real quiet. When it came time for the sermon, I listened more closely than usual.

The entrance is nearly clear and we're ready to move our small snow mountain. Dad whips it into reverse, and we back up fifty, maybe sixty, yards. We're practically in the street. A moment later we're speeding toward our mountain, which, when we hit it, explodes with a *thoomp* and blankets our windshield. For a second, I'm startled, disoriented, but the snow eventually settles enough for me to see the gaping hole that we've made. *Cool!* Then we back up and get ready to blast again.

Another forty-five minutes and the entire lot is, in my opinion, completely clean. Scraped to the bone. Still, Dad

---

3. The best I could think of was: "My friends, life is precious. And I'm here to tell you just how precious it is."

continues to plow. I look over at him, and his tongue is tucked under his lower gum in a determined expression, as if he won't be content until every last flake has been removed. He works the plow levers—yellow for raising and lowering, black for tilt—as skillfully as a boy pushing sand with a Tonka. He doesn't need to go "rmmmm, rmmmm," though; the Jeep does that for him.

Dad is one of the most complex people I know. Ask anyone in church to describe him, and they'll probably say something about how quiet and serious he is. To me, though, Dad is the funniest person in the whole world—when he chooses to be, anyway.

Last weekend, we were eating lunch at the Holiday Inn with the Burgesons and Engbergs. Karen Burgeson, who is several years younger than her husband Larry, was joking about how someday "when Larry shrivels up" she'd have to take care of him. The remark caught everyone by surprise—especially Larry. We all sat there feeling bad that Larry would grow old before the rest of us when Dad leaned toward Larry and with a perfectly straight face said, "Larry, don't shrivel." The table roared.

Still, at times, I have to agree with the majority: Dad is most comfortable behind the scenes. If not for his music, he'd be lost in the crowd. He alternates playing the organ every other weekend with Joanne Strom and plays piano for whichever Sabbath School class needs him. I only saw him up front one time. Pastor Heglund asked him to say a few words about the new organ the church was getting. "I've only spoken up front here once before," Dad said, nervously.

"And now I remember why."

Mom, who also plays the piano,[4] is more visible. She teaches at the church school, which means she's up front every couple months leading out in Investiture or a school play or whatever else. Everyone says how her programs—always full of singing, action, and costumes—are "so creative." Mom is very audience-conscious, and the last thing she'd ever want to do is bore anyone. She's always looking for a chance to help others laugh—and for a chance to laugh herself. In fact, if I had to describe Mom in two words, one of them would be "laughing."

The other would be "crying." No one in our family has ever suffered a hurt that Mom hasn't suffered with us. When chicken pox kept me out of my kindergarten play, it also kept Mom out of *watching* me in my kindergarten play. A robot that never made it out of the factory, I had to settle for putting on my eight tin cans—two on each limb—and clanking around the house singing "Robot, robot, mechanical man. Clink, clink, clink, I'm a walking tin can." Mom sat there and cried. When Angel's broken leg ruined a whole summer of butterfly catching, Mom brought a cocoon into the house so that Angel could stand there leaning on her crutches and watch the miracle happen right before her eyes.

---

4. Mom and Dad play together regularly; Mom on piano, Dad on organ. Once, at an amateur hour, they played on the same piano. The duet was going along fine until Dad, who was playing bass clef, suddenly began sliding his hands well into the treble clef, leaving Mom with about four keys to play. "Chuck, stop that!" you could see her say. The whole church howled with delight.

I'm aware that most moms feel their kids' joys and struggles. Mom just seems to do it more than her fair share.

Angel and I are just your typical Adventist kids. People in church enjoy pointing out how different we are. "You two are total opposites," they exclaim, while we stand there and wonder what they want us to do about it. It's not like we're adopted. I wasn't, anyway. But we're the same in some ways, too, more ways than people think. We both like to eat artichokes dunked in mayonnaise and Oreos dunked in milk, and we both laugh our heads off every time we watch *Snowball Express*. And we love each other. True, we don't always show this love; it's kind of our little secret, hidden amidst arguments over whose turn it is to do the dishes and what to watch on TV—*Star Search* or *The Great KX Hole-in-One Show*, my favorite. But the truth is, I'd do anything for Angel.

Two summers ago, Mom and Dad were in town and we were playing croquet at the lake cottage when a huge wind came up. ("It was practically a tornado!" we told Mom and Dad later that evening.) I grabbed Angel's hand and dragged her toward Orlo Gilbert's cottage next door. The wind—and now rain—were so strong that we could barely run against it. Without me, Angel probably would have been swept away. We reached Orlo's door just as small branches began to fly. "Well, what are you two doing outside?" exclaimed Orlo, yanking us in the door. For the next hour, we watched the storm run its course from Orlo's living room, where we sat wrapped in blankets and drinking 7UP. That day I felt more like a big brother than ever before. And it felt great.

Scraaaape. Snowplows and asphalt sound terrible together. Every hint of a snowflake has been removed from the parking lot, and our work here is finally done. A ten-foot-high bank is all that's left, a living testimony to our ambition, perseverance, and good will. Until it melts.

On the way home, I notice that we're slowing down at Mrs. Young's place. Sure enough, the left blinker's on. I don't really feel like plowing out another driveway, but now is hardly the time to complain about it. If it were anyone else's driveway, I'd have a legitimate protest. Like if it were the McTaggarts—they have two strong boys perfectly capable of shoveling out their own driveway. But Mrs. Young is different. She needs us.

Mrs. Young is 95 years old, and she lives alone. She's lived alone for a long, long time, says Mom. Her husband left her way back when, and a few years ago her son shot himself through the head. Her tiny white house has a tiny white garage, in which she keeps her giant black car, a '42 DeSoto. Dad says it's a classic. Mrs. Young will drive it to church tomorrow if she can get out of the driveway, and that's what we're helping her to do.

Frankly, Mrs. Young scares me a little. At church, she sits in the very back, and never once has she smiled at me as we exit out the middle aisle. Last year, I even took her a carnation for Mother's Day Sabbath, and *still* she didn't smile. Must be because of her birthday. A couple years ago, she mentioned to Mom that she had never had a birthday party in her whole life. One Sunday afternoon later that year, Mom swung by Mrs. Young's house, escorted her out to the van, and drove her to our house where Aletha Olson, Vern and Nettie Momb, and a few others were waiting with a big cake. Mom said Mrs. Young smiled that day, but I wasn't there, so I didn't see it.

"OK, pal, one more pass and then we're done." It's Dad. I haven't even been paying attention. Mrs. Young's driveway looks pretty good. She doesn't come out to thank us, but one of her curtains is pulled back a little, and I can tell she's watching.

Dad spins the steering wheel to the right, cuts the Jeep back into the street, and clears the remaining snow chunks off the driveway on our way home. A few hours later, our stomachs full of vegetable stew and fresh baked bread, we're sprawled by the fire having a discussion about the name of the puppy we're going to get in Alexandria on Sunday. West Highland White Terriers are small dogs, so I've suggested "Napoleon"—"Nappy," for short. Angel has suggested "Dairy," which has no meaning whatsoever. She just likes the sound of it.

Just as things start to get hostile,[5] Dad goes upstairs and returns with two bars of Ivory soap for us to carve. Within the first minute, I've accidentally cracked my bar in two and have to be content with watching Angel carve hers. "Oh, man, this is *fun*," she says every few minutes, just to annoy me. I'm about to steal her bar and hide it when Mom calls from upstairs, where she's been on the

5. We ended up using Mom's suggestion: "Que-será-será"—"Casey," for short. It suited me fine—anything but "Dairy."

phone for the past five minutes.

"Kids, come say Hi to Grandma and Grandpa."

"You go first," says Angel, giggling. "I'm making something neat."

I scamper upstairs and talk to Grandma and Grandpa, who ask what I've been doing this week.

Oh, not too much, I say.

Well, they say, surely you must have done something this week.

Of course I've done *something*. But nothing really spectacular. I'm just busy being a kid. What's there to tell?

Assigned Seating

Like many Adventist families, my family of four remembered the Sabbath day *together*. We woke up on Sabbath morning together, we ate our traditional Sabbath breakfast (cinnamon rolls, eggs, and grapefruit) together, we drove to church together, and most important, we *sat* in church together.

Of course we sat in church together. Where I grew up, church time was family time—one of those unwritten laws that most families followed and one that mine was not about to break. Angel and I knew very well that Mom and Dad expected us to find them after Sabbath School and sit with them in church. And year after year we did.

My family sat in a row[1] about halfway up in the left section of the sanctuary. The Burgesons sat just behind us; the McTaggarts in the middle of the right section; the Nelsons and Umbers just ahead of them; and the Kleins well up front in the

---

1. I use the word "row" because I've never liked the word "pew."

third row. And so, much like first graders in their assigned seats, each family in my church sat in the same row every week. The church service itself seemed to flow better with all of us in our proper places. Because our church was small (90 attendees when it hadn't snowed too hard the night before), everyone knew to stay out of another family's spot.

Unfortunately, we had an occasional problem—visitors. One Sabbath during the prelude, I watched a visiting family stride down the main aisle and sit smack dab in the third row on the right—the Kleins' row! I couldn't believe my eyes. The Kleins had sat in that row every Sabbath for years. That was *their* spot, and now someone else had taken it. *What will happen?* I wondered.

A few minutes later, I watched the Kleins themselves enter the sanctuary, walk down front briskly, pause, conference together for a moment, reverse direction, and sink slowly and bewilderedly into the fifth row. I felt sorry for the Kleins. All those years, all that time invested in their own row, and some hotshot family of five, probably from Fargo, brutally bumps them two rows back.

I waited and waited for one of the church elders to leap off the platform, scold the thieving family, and order them to switch seats with the Kleins. But no one did a thing, and I felt just sick for my friends.[2]

---

2. I recently visited my old church in Detroit Lakes and noticed that the Kleins were sitting in a completely different row, even farther from their old third row. I guess they never recovered from having their row stolen. They probably float from row to row each Sabbath, in a sort of helpless limbo.

Now forcing a family out of their assigned row in church is bad. But not half as bad as when one family member decides not to sit with the rest of his family.

One Sabbath when I was eight, I bounded up the stairs from Sabbath school, slowed to a trot in the lobby, got a drink, tip-toed quietly into the sanctuary, and as usual checked to see whether my parents were there yet. As I panned the room, I noticed that Larry, Jac, and Eric were not sitting with their families, but instead were sitting in metal folding chairs and leaning them against the back wall where Bob the soundman sat. My friends looked cool leaning back in those chairs, and I decided to get my own folding metal chair, join them in back, and be cool too.

Cool we were. Leaning against the wall with our little arms crossed. Whispering about the Vikings' new running back. Making funny faces at the toddlers in the back row. Playing "Paper, Rock, Scissors." We were so cool that some of the people in the back few rows began to watch us and talk among themselves. I figured they were probably saying things like "Those boys sure are cool." One of them even pointed at us.

I think this feeling of coolness began to diminish a bit when, between the announcements and the opening hymn, I saw Dad, who had been seated with Mom and Angel, rise from his row and look in my direction. Since I knew there weren't many things that would make Dad get up during church service, I sensed something was wrong. As Dad neared the back of the sanctuary and aimed for our area, I began to feel terribly guilty. When he got within a few feet of me, I knew that I had sinned.

"Come up by us, pal," he said gently. I tilted my chair forward, mumbled goodbye to my friends,[3] followed Dad back to our usual row, and sat down between Angel and Mom. Angel handed me a raisin, and Mom began to scratch my head, and though I wouldn't admit it at the time, I was kind of glad to be back up front with them where I belonged. Somehow, feeling loved was even cooler than feeling cool.

---

3. A little later, my friends got similar invitations to sit with their families.

Downstairs

Early, in my little church in Minnesota, I learned the difference between upstairs and downstairs. Upstairs was holy; downstairs was not. Upstairs boasted the sanctuary and the Sabbath School rooms—places conducive to quiet reflection. Downstairs countered with the kitchen and the fellowship hall—places conducive to remote-controlled cars.

I also learned that a church member could be transformed from reverence to rowdiness simply by going downstairs. Take Virgil Krogstad, for example. Upstairs, Virgil Krogstad[1] was a true gentleman—holding the door open for ladies young and old and greeting guests with a hearty handshake. But, downstairs, only eight hours later, Virgil Krogstad would battle any man, woman, or child for the last seat in a game of musical chairs. And, because Virgil Krogstad was a rather stout Norwegian with good hip action, he usually got that last seat.

---

1. His was one of those names that didn't sound complete unless you said the whole thing—Virgil Krogstad.

Which brings me to the subject of church socials.

If the 1970s Adventist church service was too stiff for some, the 1970s Adventist church social more than made up for it. Saturday night socials were held in the fellowship hall about once per quarter, and though they were well-attended, we knew we mustn't have too many of them. Something as fun as a church social should be enjoyed, but with moderation.

Usually, a church social was a game night[2]; sometimes, an amateur hour.[3] But one Sabbath, the announcement lady said the following week's church social would be (she paused for effect) an Investment Fair. "And don't forget to bring your white elephants," she said with a wink.

This announcement thoroughly confused me. *What's an Investment Fair?* I wondered. *Who owns a white elephant? And how would we get it downstairs?*

On the drive home, Mom explained "Investment Fair" and "white elephant" to Angel and me. Excited about the concept, I asked Dad whether we had any white elephants to sell at the Investment Fair. He said we did. But they weren't white. And they weren't elephants.

Eight weeks earlier Casey, our West Highland White

---

2. Balloon darts, mini golf, pie-eating contests—games that didn't take up much room as our fellowship hall was small. Once, someone set up a volleyball net, leaving a mere eighteen inches between the top of the net and the ceiling.

3. A dreaded evening for children whose parents encouraged them to do an act because "It'll be so cute!" (Dressing up like pirates and singing "The Erie Canal" with the Burgeson kids comes to mind.)

Terrier, had given birth to five black puppies (compliments of a mangy black mutt up the road). These puppies were healthy, adorable, and impossible to sell. Hence, Dad's idea for an Investment Fair project: *a puppy auction.*

Saturday night came. Fifteen minutes into the auction, we were still waiting for an opening bid. Seeing our drooping heads, Mom hatched an alternate idea, one that wouldn't rid us of our puppies but would raise money for the church. *Puppy races.* We decided to try it.

Under Dad's orders, Angel and I dashed around the hall, asking appalled faces which puppy they'd like to bet on and how much they'd like to bet. No one dared respond . . . that is, until the pastor himself put five dollars on Puppy Two. Then the dam burst.

"I'll put fifteen dollars on Puppy Four," shouted the head elder.

"Puppy One for ten bucks—no, make that twelve," said the Sabbath School superintendent.

"Give me Puppy Five," said Virgil Krogstad. "Here's ten dollars."

Moments later all bets had been placed, and the first puppy race in our church's history was set to begin. Dad found a long jump rope and laid it in a big circle on the floor. Mom and Angel labeled the five yapping puppies with construction paper and corralled them into the middle of the circle.

"On your marks . . ." I said. "Get set . . . Go!"

The puppies huddled together. Not one moved. Then . . .

"Go. Go little puppy," whispered 75-year-old Mildred Odegard.

One puppy perked up and began to wander toward Mildred. Instantly a dozen church members dove to the edges of the rope circle. "Come on, number two! You can do it!"

"Here puppy, puppy, puppy. No—not you! *You!*"

"Come on, boy. Come on!"

I'd never seen anything like it, and I probably never will again. Half the church lying prostrate on the floor, pleading with the confused puppies to take a few more small steps.

After forty-five seconds of bedlam, Puppy Two scampered across the rope into Barb Halvorsen's arms. As the puppy licked her face, Barb looked as though she had won millions. (She hadn't, of course; all the money went to the church.)

The others rose to their feet, some more slowly than others, some much more slowly than others, and began to collect themselves. Never in their lives had they laughed so hard. I heard one lady say her sides hurt, and I felt bad for her because everyone else was having such a good time.

The next Sabbath, when I saw Virgil Krogstad in the church lobby, I wanted to talk and laugh with him about the puppy races. But I figured since we were upstairs, I'd better not.

Stories

When I was growing up, few things were as exciting as the stories Mom read to Angel and me on my little blue bed upstairs every night. Now, granted, some nights I would have much rather been, say, in the living room watching *The Six Million Dollar Man* than in my bedroom reading *Morris and the Merry-Go-Round*, but, for the most part, I liked our nightly routine. . . .

Just before dark, Dad would throw me one last pass, a 60-yard bomb. With a leaping grab in the end zone with no time remaining, the game was won and we would strut up to the house. Inside, Mom would be applying a bitter formula to Angel's fingernails so she would stop biting them.[1]

"It's getting late, Chuck," Mom would say.

---

1. We both got the stuff for a while—until the night Mom was rocking Angel to sleep, and Mom, thinking Angel *was* asleep, yawned, at which point, Angel, who wasn't asleep at all, jammed her whole hand into Mom's mouth, and we didn't have to have the formula anymore.

"Yup, it is," Dad would say.

And, turning to us, he would utter that totally predictable phrase. "Shadrach, Meshach, and to bed we go!"

"Nooooo," we would say.

"Yeeesssss," he would say.

And then he would chase us up the red stairs. Casey, barking idiotically, would join in. And our cat—who had no name—would scamper out of the way[2] as we galloped into my room. Except sometimes, Dad didn't quite make it into my room. I had a pull-up bar across my door and about twenty percent of our chases ended with him *whapping* his head, which quickly changed the mood, both his and ours. Then I would change into my yellow pajamas, which I don't have anymore, and we would wait for Mom.

Mom would carry in a stack of books and sit between Angel and me and read to us. She read us books of all kinds. There were a few standbys, though, such as Dr. Seuss books, which were especially fun to read out loud. "Hand, hand, fingers, thumb. One thumb, one thumb drumming on a drum. Dum ditty, dum ditty, dum dum dum."

---

2. This was the same cat that liked to sleep on my parents' bed. One night, very late, the phone rang. Because Dad was closer to the phone, Mom just waited for him to get it. She says she could hear him saying "Hello? Hello?" but, for some strange reason, the phone kept ringing. "Hello, Nashes," said Dad as the phone continued to ring. At this point, Mom turned over to discover that my dad had grabbed the cat rather than the phone. "Hello? Hello?" he continued to say into the dumbfounded cat. For years afterward, the cat steered well clear of my dad—in case the phone should ring.

Sometimes, when Angel had gone to sleep early, Mom would treat me to sports books such as *Baseball Players Do Amazing Things*. The first time we read *Baseball Players Do Amazing Things*, I became convinced that life really was worth living. Here they were—the greatest baseball moments of all time: Babe Ruth's called shot, Willie Mays's over-the-shoulder grab in deep center field, Jackie Robinson's stealing home. My favorite story was the time the St. Louis Cardinals sent Eddie Haskell, a 4′9″ midget, up to bat. Haskell walked every time; no pitcher could find his strike zone. Mom and I laughed and laughed. The only thing, I decided, that could possibly be better than this collection would be *Football Players Do Amazing Things*, but Mom said they didn't make that one and I didn't dare get my hopes up. I knew I should be content with what I had.

One Christmas morning, Angel and I raced down the stairs—not as hastily as kids who *hadn't* opened their main gifts the night before, but not slowly either: Christmas stockings should never be underestimated—and my dream came true. There it was: the newly published *Football Players Do Amazing Things*. I couldn't speak; it was almost too much to behold. *Did I deserve such a gift?* I asked myself.

Deciding that yes, I did deserve such a gift, I began to delicately turn the pages, not allowing myself to read the stories, just skimming the titles. There they were—the greatest, most amazing moments in professional football history: Tom Dempsey's 63-yard field goal, Gayle Sayer's six-touchdown afternoon, Norm Van Brocklin's passing frenzy. *Amazing!* We read one story per night for two weeks, then we started over again.

The only negative about the book was that the lone mention of the Minnesota Vikings was when defensive lineman Jim Marshall scooped up a fumble and ran sixty yards—the wrong way. The photo showed a San Francisco 49er congratulating Jim Marshall on scoring points for the wrong team. I couldn't even imagine how Jim Marshall felt. Sometimes I went to bed thinking about his wrong-way run. *How could he do that? Didn't he know he was going the wrong way? Why didn't the other Vikings— the smaller, faster ones—catch up and tackle him?* And, as I lay there trying to deal with what happened, I couldn't help but wonder if maybe Jim Marshall himself was lying in bed that same night, reliving the play and asking himself, How could I be so *dumb*?

Still, as great as *Football Players Do Amazing Things* was, it didn't make me feel as good inside as the last, and most often-opened, set of books: Arthur Maxwell's big blue *Bible Story* collection. Angel and I knew very little about Arthur Maxwell, but we knew everything about his books: David would always be wearing yellow, baby Moses wouldn't have to wait in the bulrushes for long, Sampson would lose his secret strength—but how could he *not* feel Delilah cutting his hair? If someone were cutting *my* hair, I would feel it.

Angel's favorite story was "Jesus and the Children." She could recite the whole thing. "Suffer the little children to come unto Me," she and Mom said in unison. "*And forbid them not.*" Sometimes Warren and Eleanor

Engberg[3] would come over to play Rook with Mom and Dad—"Good night! I can't believe we didn't make our bid"—and they would come upstairs to hear Angel's talent. I didn't mind all the fuss. Eleanor always scratched my head while Angel recited.

Once or twice a night, Angel would get Mom off on a subject that didn't interest me in the least—such as Did Jesus collect bugs?—and I would put my head back and count the blue soldiers and red drums on my wallpaper[4] and think about these stories and wonder what *I* would do if they were threatening to throw me into a fiery furnace or a den of lions.

Sometimes, after Mom and Angel left, I would turn on the light, flip open the front cover, and study the picture of the Flood. It was a powerful picture; I thought about it a lot. I thought about the people pounding on the door of Noah's Ark as the waves swept around them. But, mostly, I thought about the animals that didn't make it inside. The people being drowned I could understand. They blew it. But the animals? What chance did they have?

"Hey, everybody! Come on! Your Story Hour's on!"

Our routine of reading Bible storybooks during the week

3. Once in school I wrote a paragraph about Warren and Eleanor, except I spelled their names "Worn and Elner," and of course Mom had to bring the paragraph to church and show them. Oh, how they laughed while I wondered what the big deal was.
4. I used a similar technique in church when the pastor was talking about a subject that didn't interest me, except there I looked at the ceiling and counted knotholes.

was interrupted every weekend by something just as good—listening to Bible story tapes. Aunt Sue and Uncle Dan dropped by Friday night and Saturday afternoon and occasionally on Sunday morning to tell us about the "Hero of Cave City," "Strangers in the Night," "Maggie and the Big Yellow Dogs," and other people who lived more exciting lives than we did.

We had several boxes containing hundreds of stories—a Bible one on the back; a "today" one on the front—but most of the stories we never got to; we found five or six we liked and kept rotating them. What was the point of risking a half hour on a potentially boring story when you had five stories guaranteed to please you every single time?

Once, Mom came in to her bedroom—which is where we sat and listened to the stories—and tried to talk us into some new stories. "Here's one about a tiger," she said.

"No, Mom, we like *these*," we told her. She laughed and told us we were silly and went back downstairs.

She left the tape laying beside the machine, though, so we decided to pop it in. "Mumba and the Tiger" wasn't bad, really. It was about an African boy who played the flute and who didn't get to go with the men to hunt the man-eating tiger that had been ravaging their village. "No, Mumba, you stay home with the women and children," they had told him. So he kicked around the village until he heard the scream.

"Mumba," someone cried. "The tiger is about to eat the Nanny and her baby." Before long, Mumba had his flute to his mouth and the piercing notes were enough to make the man-eater back off, the pied piper in reverse. It was a slow backing off, though, and Mumba began to worry about how long he could play.

Oh, my lips are so dry, thought Mumba. *But I must keep playing my flute or the tiger will eat me.* Mumba consistently managed to play his flute long enough to drive out the tiger and save the Nanny and her baby. Sometimes, just for variety, I wished that Mumba's lips *would* get too dry and the tiger would eat him. But it never happened; Mumba's lips managed to remain just moist enough. And I felt bad for thinking such a terrible thought.

"Goodbye everybody! See ya again next week!" When the story finished, the theme music began—our cue to jump on Mom and Dad's bed. I'm not sure why we always jumped on the bed when the music began. It just seemed like the thing to do.

Story's over. Catchy music begins. Jump on bed like maniacs. Music ends. Rewind tape five seconds. Jump on bed some more. Mom hears racket upstairs. Mom comes upstairs. Mom flings open door. Mom sees kids jumping on bed. Mom starts jumping on bed too.

I'm kidding, of course. Mom didn't jump on the bed until after we had gone.

Rules

Growing up, I listened to a lot of Adventists my age complain about their childhood. They groaned about all the rules their parents and teachers "crammed down their throats," and how they could "never measure up," and how God was presented as "out to get you," and how growing up Adventist was "frustrating" enough to make them want to ditch this "legalistic" church.

Rules were a very minor part of my childhood. Oh, sure, there was the occasional worry that I was doing something I shouldn't be doing—or that I wasn't doing something I *should* be doing.[1]

---

1. Once Mom told me that we were supposed to drink eight glasses of water a day. I grabbed a Dixie cup, filled it up, downed it, filled it up again, downed it, filled it up again. . . . "Not all at once, silly!" she said, but I was in a rhythm. By cup five, I was waterlogged—a snorkeler who had gone down a little too far. But only three cups from being a healthy person, I continued to drink. Six cups, seven cups, seven and a third, breath, seven and two-thirds, breath, *eight*. I went straight to bed with a colossal stomachache.

But these worries didn't dominate my early years, as they apparently did for other kids.

My only real struggle with rules was when the Minnesota Vikings played televised games on Sabbath. (They normally played on Sundays—and occasionally even won.) The rest of the family would be outside making snow angels or upstairs taking a nap, and I would sit on the living room sofa in front of a blank TV screen *just sure* that I was missing the greatest game in NFL history.

Oh, my! What an unbelievable catch! Touchdown, Minnesota! . . . Jack, I don't know when I've ever seen anything so exciting. That Ahmad Rashad is really something, isn't he?

Yes, Hank, he is. What a terrific game this has been to watch!

One game I decided that since my mind was already sinning, my eyes might as well join in. I crept to the TV. Out, then in, went the knob—out just long enough for me to catch the score: Philadelphia 6, Minnesota 3.

And I felt so guilty.

But, aside from such brief, tormenting lapses into delinquency, I enjoyed a relatively worry-free Adventist childhood. Part of the reason was that I had a dad who hadn't had a pleasant experience with rules. Dad didn't talk much about his younger days, so I never got a real good reading on exactly what had happened. But Mom, who was glad to talk about anyone's younger days, told me that Dad had been kicked out of the academy for breaking the rules—no questions asked, no help offered—and that she thought it had really hurt him inside. He ended up graduating at home.

I couldn't believe it. They kicked out Dad? What a sham!

As it turned out, though, some good had come from the academy's devotion to high standards and low tolerance: Dad wasn't about to treat us the same way. While Angel and I had plenty of rules and expectations, we knew that rules and expectations would always yield to acceptance and a second chance—the perfect environment for wanting to do good.

Plus, Dad and Mom spent very little time looking for new sins that we hadn't yet realized—new truths for the purpose of making life difficult. So, while others debated whether or not Santa Claus was evil,[2] Dad would be at Target spending his own money on presents for poor kids in the church. Then he would pull on his reds and whites, the ideal means for giving anonymously, and drive around town, handing out Stomper trucks and Strawberry Shortcake dolls to children who had never received either.

So we didn't do a lot of worrying about behavior—ours or others', though the latter could be an extremely exhilarating activity, particularly when it involved the pastor's family. There simply wasn't time for worrying. We had too much living to do.

---

2. If you play with the letters enough, you can spell "Satan," you know.

Consistency

There was, in my childhood church, a special group of people who might not have known how much I liked them. Relics from yesteryear, living testimonies to bygone wars (II, I, Civil, Revolutionary), born even before Ellen White died, they quietly accepted their final label: old people.

To visitors and to teenagers, the old people in our church might have seemed unexciting, scary. But to me, a little kid, they were one thing and one thing only: consistent.

First, they were always on time. Road conditions that kept the postman in his toasty warm bed couldn't keep the old people away from church. Even if they had to leave at half past seven, *even if they knew that the sermon was going to be an audiotape,*[1]

1. Besides being used on blizzard weekends, audiotapes were used as punishment against those who didn't go to camp meeting. One of the elders would give an introduction, telling how much this message had meant to him and how he hoped it did the same for us, then give a nod to Bob back at the sound equipment. The problem with tapes was that you were never sure where to look. Most just watched the pulpit because that's what they were used to. Some even said "Amen" to the parts they especially liked.

they'd be there. The few times my family arrived early, I'd see them sitting in the empty sanctuary reviewing their Sabbath school quarterlies while someone set up the screen for Mission Spotlight.

Second, they always had time for me. I didn't have to say something exciting just to hold their attention. They would just stand in the lobby after church and listen to me jabber about my new bike or my loose tooth or the batch of kittens our cat just had (one died) as much as I liked. Sometimes they would ask boring questions, such as What did I learn in Sabbath school that morning?, but mostly I enjoyed talking with them. When everyone else was too busy to listen, they hung on my every word.

Now while I liked most all the old people in our church, a few were extra-special:

Harold and Aletha Olson. Our adopted grandparents, Harold and Aletha lived in a farmhouse across the street and up a steep driveway from our lake cottage. On Sabbath afternoons in the fall, we pulled on our jeans jackets and went up to visit. Harold told good stories about animals. A few minutes into our conversation, Aletha would slip into the kitchen and return with rhubarb pie, sweet rolls, hot cocoa, and other morale-builders. We always acted surprised that she had made something—"oh, Aletha, you really shouldn't have"—but the truth is, if Aletha had ever returned from the kitchen with anything less than a bakery, we would have become disoriented. Our friends on the hill spoiled us rotten—and we loved every minute of it.

Clarence Johnson. I really didn't know Clarence very well, but for some reason, I identified with him. He always seemed to get the short end of the stick. One night for amateur hour, Clarence dusted off his old beat-up violin, carved away on it for five minutes, bowed, and sat down to warm applause. He looked pleased. Unfortunately for Clarence, the next act was the talented Gaylord Odegard and his accordion. As the rich melodies of Gaylord's accordion filled the fellowship hall and inspired people to cheer and clap along vigorously, Clarence looked as if he wished he hadn't brought along his old violin after all. I felt bad for Clarence; I knew what it was like to be upstaged. It wasn't fun.

Dorothy Momb. Dorothy, who baby-sat my sister Angel at our house for one school year, was particularly alert and versatile, which came in handy. You *had* to be alert and versatile to baby-sit my sister.[2] But above all, Dorothy was supportive. She was always telling me how I was going to become a pastor someday. "Oh, you'll make such a fine pastor," she said. Even though I didn't *want* to be a pastor (I wanted to be the coach of the Minnesota Vikings and maybe play a little too), I was glad that Dorothy thought I *could* be a pastor. Even with all the dumb things I did, she thought I could be a pastor. She believed in me, which was all I really

---

2. I'd come home from school and Angel would have Dorothy's hair in curlers and her *Heaven Is For Kids* album blaring in the background. Once, Dorothy was chasing Angel down the stairs and she lost her footing and began to roll, a human tumbleweed. "Dorothy Momb!" yelled Angel. "Are you OK, Dorothy Momb?" Dorothy was fine—just a little dazed. It had been a while since she'd descended the stairs that quickly.

ever needed from her.

Believing in me was all I really ever needed from any of them. And it's what I got.

Church School

Church school has many advantages. One of the good things about our school is that the teacher doesn't have to hurry around so much because there's not as many kids having questions at the same time, and the younger kids that have questions can ask kids that are older than them.

Some of the things I like to do in church school are go to the library downtown, have Bible quizzes, and have movies. I like the stories we read like Unleashed, The Pearl, *and* The Little Missionary Truck That Could Do Anything.

I really don't see why all the kids from other schools say school is so boring because I think it is really fun. I don't think school is boring. The subjects aren't boring, the playtime isn't boring. I'm in a church and in a church school they teach you to be thankful that you have a church school to go to. —Andy Nash, 9

The Detroit Lakes Seventh-day Adventist Church School is just down the hall from the Detroit Lakes Seventh-day Adventist Church, across from the bathrooms and the water fountain. We have two classrooms, which on the weekends we allow the adults to use for Sabbath School, but we hate when they open our desks—we have personal stuff in there. Can't they bring their own pencils?

In the late 70s, there was a movement among the school board to update the name of our school. Not only was the Detroit Lakes Seventh-day Adventist Church School a cumbersome name,[1] but many thought it might perplex some non-Adventists in town who wanted to send their child to a country Christian school like on *Little House on the Prairie*, but who didn't know what to think about the name "Seventh-day Adventist."

"Do you think they will try to convert Sarah to their religion?" a hypothetical wife would ask her hypothetical husband.

"Well, I don't know," he would say. "Do you?"

And then, deciding that the risks were too high, they would send Sarah to public school instead.

But, if the school had a less conspicuous name, Sarah's parents might be more likely to send her there. They came up with several alternatives. The two finalists were Meadow Vista Christian School and Mountain Vista[2] Christian School. (Everyone

---

1. Rule of thumb: A school should have fewer words in its name than students in its classrooms.

2. "Mountain Vista" referred to Detroit Mountain, a small ski hill that could, in fact, be viewed from the school's east window. I began skiing on Detroit Mountain when I was only three. I didn't use ski poles; I just put my hands on my knees and made "lots of turns," as Dad had instructed. Unfortunately, my aptitude for skiing technique was canceled out by a lack of skiing fashion. Mom probably didn't think it mattered that the combination of my long hair and light blue hood made me look like a girl. But it did matter. All night long, people exclaimed, "Oh, look at that little girl skiing down that hill!", and to this day, I avoid light blue hoods.

liked the word "vista.") After hours of heated debate, the board could not reach a consensus. Plus, some key members couldn't quite shake the feeling that by dropping the word "Adventist," we might be forfeiting our heritage. So they threw out the whole idea and decided to retain the present name: the Detroit Lakes Seventh-day Adventist Church School.

I was disappointed. "Hello, Detroit Lakes Seventh-day Adventist Church School, may I help you?" was a mouthful when the hall phone rang. We would race to get it.

By "we," I mean the cast of the church school: the big kids (grades 5-8), taught by Mr. Rogers, and the little kids (grades 1-4), taught by Mom. But I didn't call her Mom; I called her Mrs. Nash. (I wanted everything to be as fair as possible.) Mrs. Nash made us write us a lot of "themes," no matter how much we rolled our eyes and complained because, she said, we'd be grateful later on. She'd write a topic sentence on the board, such as "Every student in my classroom has good qualities" and then ask us to finish it.

"Do we really have to write another theme, Mrs. Nash?"

"Yes, you do," she said, laughing. "Now get to it."

Every student in my classroom has good qualities. Jac is good at football and baseball. But Larry is good at soccer and basketball. Micky helps people and is good at art. Jenny helps people, too, but Jenny is good at naming capitals. Debbie shares and obeys the teacher. Rocky has good sportsmanship and shares too. And last of all, Val is good at, Val is good at, I can't think of what Val is good at. I suppose Val is good at Bible. So everybody in the room is good at something except, oh forget it.—Andy Nash, 7

Actually, Val was good at a lot of things. I just teased her because she could take it. Learning to take it comes with the territory in a multi-grade school. If you don't, you're in for a miserable year. The big kids would see to that.

The big kids got to do a lot of things. They got to repeat the JMV law, which meant that they would be a servant of God and a friend to man, walk softly in the sanctuary, keep a song in their hearts, and go on God's errands. It sounded neat the way they said it. Our pledge was more straightforward: be true, be kind, be faithful, be obedient, and things like that. We recited our pledges every Monday morning in the junior room downstairs—boys sat on the left, girls on the right. We didn't have to sit that way; we wanted to. Occasionally a boy would stray to the right, which was disappointing. But he always found his way back, and we accepted him with open arms.

I never strayed to the right. Even if I had wanted to stray, I wouldn't have—Mom would see me and discover my secret: Girls weren't as gross as I said they were. I sat in the left front so I could see. Being the shortest student in the whole school could, I suppose, have been a real downer. No second grade boy likes to have a five-inch gap between his height line on the wall and the other lines—two of which belonged to second grade *girls*, Debbie and Rocky.

Most everyone had a nickname in church school, and it didn't take long for me to get mine: "Shorts." Eric "Erki" Klein, the biggest kid in the school, made it up. Everyone laughed their heads off when he said it. At first, I was embarrassed, but after a few days, I got used to the name and even grew to like it. "Way to go, Shorts," the big kids would yell on the playground, and it made me want to run all the faster. With a name like "Shorts," the only place you could go was up.

Erki sat behind me. He pulled my chair back half way and let me try to balance it in mid-air during announcements. We had to stand, though, to say the Pledge of Allegiance[3] while two students—never me—unfolded the flag that two other students—never me—had folded perfectly the previous Friday. "See, Andy," they had said earlier that year, "only the blue section is supposed to show. Want to try again?" I didn't. Who cares if the stripes showed a little? I mean, were we suddenly prone to a Russian attack just because I hadn't folded the American flag perfectly?

Pastor Heglund, who had slipped in the back door during the flag-unfolding, then came forward for our worship talk. A small man with white hair combed straight back, Pastor Heglund was a true "servant of God, friend to man." His voice was soothing as he shared his thought, which often included a selection from Paul Harvey. It was hard, though, to fully enjoy Pastor Heglund's talk because all we were thinking about was when he would ask us to raise our hands. He *always* asked us to raise our hands, a scaled-down altar call in which everyone was expected to participate. "And so," said Pastor Heglund, "[Someone] never forgot her ex-

---

3. We were careful to emphasize the words "under God" to make up for all the public school kids who we heard were no longer saying "under God." What was this country coming to anyway?

perience with [something], and she promised herself that she would [positive act] the next chance she got. How many of you want to do the same thing?" And we'd all raise our hands.

After worship we raced up the red stairs, the little kids to their classroom, the big kids to theirs; we would see them again at noon hour. "Bye, Erki," I said.

"See ya, Shorts," he said and laughed his way into his classroom.

"OK," said Mrs. Nash. "I'd like you to spend a little time working on your next vocabulary assignment, and while you do I'll be reviewing your Iowa Basic Skills results with you individually . . ." And for the next few hours, we became smarter people.

By noon hour, though, we were ready to give our expanding minds a break. A herd of elephants down the stairs, we scarfed down our sandwiches as fast as we could[4] and gathered for our noon hour activity, which was highly dependent upon the weather. The first few weeks of winter you couldn't keep us inside even if you tried. Snow meant sledding, and sledding meant Indian Hill. It took ten minutes to walk there—we passed the time by whipping snowballs at each other: "Hey, you guys, stop throwing ice! That hurt!"—but it was worth the journey.

Indian Hill was the king of sledding runs: dangerously steep, probably 88 or 89 degrees, and as fast as you'd ever want to go. As soon as you hurtled off the top, you had to

---

4. Larry always got to have white bread on his sandwich.

begin braking with your hands; otherwise, you'd fly into the far woods someplace, never to be heard from again. They'd find you during a building project next century, your face forever frozen in elation. Not a bad way to go out, really.

Still, below-zero temperatures and ice chunks that get inside your mittens and freeze your wrists lose appeal after a while, and by January we were back inside playing floor hockey in the fellowship hall, unless it was being used by the Dorcas Society, in which case we were upstairs playing Risk, Monopoly, or Electric Football.

Electric football, a game in which your team of little plastic players moves to the rhythm of a vibrating board, was unmatched in excitement. You never knew where your man was going to go. He could be racing up the field, just five yards from the endzone—then, without warning, do the hokey pokey, turn himself around, and dash the other direction. Unfortunately, the game was also unmatched in controversy. For a player to be tackled, his sliding base had to be touched by another player's sliding base. But sometimes the ball carrier was vibrating along so fast that it was tough to tell whether contact had been made.

"He touched."

"No, he didn't."

"Yes, he did. Debbie, did you see it? Tell him he touched."

By early March, most of the snow had melted and we were ready to let our plastic football teams have some time off—they had worked hard—and play the game ourselves. Mr. Rogers played with us. He was all-time quarterback— friend one minute, foe the next. He'd bark the signals, just like on TV. "Down . . . set . . . hike!" and we'd all run around like maniacs, doing everything we could to lose our defender.

On this day, though, Mr. Rogers had to run a quick errand in town. The minute he left, John Umber surprised all of us by suggesting that we switch from touch football to tackle football, which he described as a "real man's game."

"Hey, yeah!" said a couple kids.

"Hey, yeah!" said a couple more.

I didn't want to be the only wimp. "Hey, yeah!" I said.

Before I knew what was happening, the kickoff was sailing right at me. I fled five yards to the right. The wind compensated.

"It's yours, Shorts!" someone yelled.

The ball arrived just a split second before the kickoff team. I cut left, an end run, but Danny had closed off the corner. A couple of my teammates tried to block, but they were steamrolled by the enthusiastic mob. It's not every day you get to smear a second grader.

Reversing field, I dodged Jenny, then shook off Jac. Just as I was gaining confidence, I saw him—Erki!

He lumbered toward me, a mountain on the move. Daylight disappeared. I hugged the ball and lowered my head . . .

Whoomp!

What had happened? I wasn't sure. My head hurt a little, but I was still standing—*still alive*. I spun around, but no one was even paying attention to me. They were all huddled around Erki, who was crawling around on his hands and knees. He seemed to be searching for something.

"You knocked his tooth out!" someone yelled.

What? Erki's tooth?

"It's his front one," said someone else. "It's bleeding!"

After school, I still couldn't believe what had happened. "It's bleeding!" had sent me bolting from the scene. For more than an hour I hid in the tall grass behind the soccer field while everyone looked for me. "Where are you, Shorts?" they called out impatiently, but I didn't answer. I didn't know what to say. Finally, I decided that if they called out just once more, I would stand up and show myself. But no one called.

I returned to class in the middle of Bible. I squeaked open the door, and everyone looked up in unison. Most of them seemed glad to see me—if they hadn't, I would have run away again. Maybe for good. A second grader can only carry so much sorrow at a time.

They told me the news. Erki was OK. He had found his tooth and *stuck it back in his mouth*. The dentist had called from downtown to say that the tooth had been saved. The roots had taken hold. Erki's parents had also called to say that he wasn't mad at me and neither were they, but that they hoped we had all learned a good lesson. We had.

Still, I felt lousy. Not just because I'd knocked out my buddy's tooth but because I'd fled, a gutless criminal at large. I could have at least stuck around long enough to help.

By 3:45, all the kids except the Stutzmans had caught their rides so I just sat on the sidewalk and watched Todd fry ants with his magnifying glass and say "Decent!" while I waited for Mom. Todd always said "Decent!" when he liked something. By the end of the year, we were all saying, "Decent!" He'd herd a few ants onto the middle of the sidewalk with his notebook, then catch the sun with his magnifying glass and execute them one by one.

"Decent!" he said. The ants didn't seem to think it was all that decent.

A few minutes later, Mrs. Nash came clicking outside, her arms full of papers to grade. Seeing her made my throat get tight, as it had been when Erki was crawling around the grass. I hadn't had a chance to talk to her about the accident, and I was anxious to get home so she could hug me while I cried.

"How about you and I swing by Dairy Queen on the way?" she said.

My throat loosened a little. The idea had potential.

"Can I get a Peanut Buster Parfait?" I asked.

"Only if I can," she said.

We hopped in the van and drove away, teacher and student, mother and son.

Other early works by Andy Nash (aged 7-9):

One day a guy in the park asked me, "What do Seventh-day Adventists believe?" They believe it's wrong to drink and smoke. They believe that we should go to church on Saturday. Seventh-day Adventists keep the Ten Commandments and are kind to people. But even people that aren't Seventh-day Adventists are still my friends.

Children and adults are not very much alike. When I want to go to football games, Mom wants to go to Tupperware parties. When I want to go to baseball games, Dad wants to haul wood. It makes me mad! I have to go to bed early. Mom and Dad get to stay up and play games. But, believe it or not, we still get along.

I am planning a camping trip to Canada with my friends. I am taking Larry, Jac, David, Eric, Todd, and Danny. We are going to fly in an airplane to Wisconsin. Then we are going to swim across Lake Superior. We are going to go around Olympic time. We are going to play hockey for the United States hockey team against Canada. And as soon as we win, which I'm sure we will, we will each drive our own car which we got for winning the hockey game. Then we will drive back to the United States and sign autographs and be very famous.

Many people have jobs that I think would be interesting. I think it would be neat to be a lifeguard and to be able to save people's lives. I'd like to be a preacher and preach to people. It would be fun to work in a nutrition store and sell people good foods to eat. I would like to be a missionary and help build churches and preach to people. I don't have time to do all of these things so I'm not going to worry about them right now.

Almost everyone knows that boys and girls like different things. Boys like to go to fun football games. Girls like to go to boring ballet stuff. When boys go to the beach they play in the water and have lots of fun. Girls lay on the beach and make fools of themselves. I wonder why girls come up with such boring things. But we both like to eat, don't we?

I am happy to say that soon I will be leaving for Iran. I am going to free the hostages. Since Iran is two and a half times bigger than Texas, I'll have plenty of places to hide. I think I'll hide in the Lake Urmia. Then I will try to get the Iranians to make a peace treaty with the U.S.A. It's fun to be a hero.

One day a small girl asked me, "What is spring?" I told her spring is when birds come back, and when flowers, grass, and leaves grow. She asked, "What are you spost to do in the spring?" I said, "Play football and baseball." "Don't you get smart with me, you know I don't like those games." I told her spring is when we play in the water, and when we get a suntan. Then she said, "I want to do all of these things except the dumb games." "If you want to all of those things, you better hurry up," I said.

My pet is the strangest animal in the world. My pet is a fun frog. I call him Freddie. We like to play basketball. The other day he beat me 62-28. He always does jump shots and I can never reach them. When I get the ball he gets on the rim of the hoop and blocks the shots. One time the Vikings came over to my house for supper. When Freddie found out they liked to eat froglegs he ran away. As soon as the Vikings left he came back and beat me in another game of basketball.

Christmas Plays

I remember thinking that the announcement hadn't done us justice.

"And last," said the man up front, "you're all invited to our church school's Christmas program this evening. It begins at—just a moment . . . OK, as your bulletin says, the program begins at 7:30. Cake and hot apple cider will be served afterward, so be sure to drop by if you can."

Stunned, I sat with my family in our regular row. *Drop by if you can?* Is this why we had canceled recess for two months? So our audience could *drop by?* I turned to Mom, the church school teacher and therefore the Christmas play director, but she seemed satisfied with the announcement. I wasn't. I wanted something more, something big, something *dramatic. . .*

"Folks? Folks? Let me have your undivided attention. I stand before you with a very special announcement. Tonight at 7:30, our fellowship hall will be graced by the eighteen elite members of the Detroit Lakes Seventh-day Adventist

Church School in their annual Christmas pageant. Their program is entitled—Joanne, could I have some soft organ music? . . . yes, there we go. Their program is entitled, "Angels and Lambs, Ladybugs and Fireflies." Now please remain calm. And please be extra cautious on your Sabbath afternoon drives. You don't want to miss this—

"Hold on, folks. I just noticed that seated among us this morning is one of our budding young stars. He's in second grade, and his acting experience includes Bible charades. What a pleasure it is to have him here! Andy Nash, would you please stand? . . ." (*applause*).

My daydream unrealized, I worried all afternoon about our Christmas play. As lead firefly, I had worked hard on my line ("Follow me, everyone!") and at turning my hidden flashlight on and off at just the right moment, and I wondered whether anyone would come to see it. Mom reminded me that Grandma and Grandpa and Uncle Paul from Lincoln and also Angel and Dad would be at the program, and I was grateful that they would be, but would anyone else?

Evening came, and then night, and the seven of us piled into the van and drove over to the church early so Mom and I could get ready and so Grandma and Grandpa could get good seats. But, when we got there, the good seats were gone.

Patiently, they sat waiting—three full rows of grandparents who had driven in from Frazee and Fargo and Sioux Falls and one set who had *flown* in from Arizona and who looked cold. Behind them, a half dozen church members puttered with their eight-millimeter cameras. *Wow*, I said to myself as Grandma lamented our late arrival. *This is bigger than I expected!*

Then a strange thing happened. No longer was I worried that not enough people would come to our Christmas play. Now I was worried that too many people would come. *This place is going to be packed by people expecting great things,* I thought. *What if I messed up my line?*

"Follow me, everyone!" It was an easy line. I had memorized it the very first week. But what if I said, "Follow everyone, me!" or "Follow everyme, one!"? What if I forgot my line altogether?

That would be disastrous. People would talk about it for months. They'd see me in the lobby after church and nod knowingly to each other. "It's him," they'd whisper. "It's the boy who ruined the Christmas play."

Petrified, I ran up the stairs—two at a time—to meet the other kids. They were nervous, too, and for the next twenty minutes we put glitter on our wings and talked about how nervous we were. One girl, Jenny, told us that she wasn't nervous at all, but she was obviously just trying to be cool. How could she not be nervous? This night had "nervous" written all over it.

By 7:20, Mom was talking to us about everything we had been through and reminding us to project. By 7:25 we were downstairs, peaking around the corner. By 7:28 we were about to die. And, then, we were on—winged and singing.

"Angels and lambs, ladybugs and fireflies told
everybody in sight

That Jesus is born in Beth-le-hem, on that
  Chri-ist-mas night.
The fireflies lit their lights so bright. The butter-
  flies and grasshoppers helped out too.
The ladybugs, cockatiels, hummingbirds, and owls
  were the bird and insect publicity crew . . ."

I got my line that Chri-ist-mas night. *Nailed it.* But, as I later learned, it wouldn't have mattered a lick if I hadn't. Christmas plays in small Adventist churches were destined to be smashing successes. A kid could foul up, freeze up, trip up, throw up—and still be a hit.

The plot of our programs, of course, changed from year to year. But the response never did: a packed house, howling laughter after every one-liner, appreciative applause after every nervous solo, and a thunderous standing ovation that clipped the end off our final number.

The night's closing scenes were always the same too: cake and cider for everyone, a surprise visit from Santa (the cue for at least one conservative family to get their coats), and the formation of roughly eighteen clusters of people hugging our little necks, remarking how they'd "never seen anything so good," and heaping onto us much more glory than we ever expected or deserved—which, for Christmas, was hardly a new concept.

Box Socials

I learned about box socials[1] on the way to one when I was eight. I was less than thrilled. "Box social" smacked of romance, and romance wasn't my thing.

My lone dabbling-in-romance had been a disaster. In a church school drawing, I had won a giant colorful Reagan/Bush election poster, which I promptly forwarded to a fourth grader named Tricia who I thought I liked. "Here you go, Tricia," I said. "Do you want this poster? I don't really want it."

I couldn't have told a bigger lie. For months I had coveted that poster as it hung beside Jimmy Carter's on the classroom wall. I had *prayed* about that poster. But what did I do when I got it? I gave it to a *girl*. Worse, I gave it to a girl who might have been a Democrat.

---

1. Box socials are evenings in which boys of all ages compete (make fools of themselves) in various events for dessert boxes prepared by girls of all ages. They are held on Valentine's weekend—or whenever the social activities coordinator thinks the church needs one.

"Oh, thanks," Tricia said politely (a bad sign) as she left to catch the bus, where she and her friends probably laughed all the way home. "He gave you *that*? Aaaahhhhaaaaa!"

And so I had little interest in participating in an event in which the prize was sharing dessert with a *girl*. "Isn't there a way I can just eat the girl's dessert without the girl?" I asked Mom, as we got out of the van. "No, Andy," she said, and I was stuck.

Oh well, I thought as I sat with Larry and Jac on the stage of the Rossman Elementary gym, which the church had rented. *I'll just sit this one out*.

"OK," said the emcee. "Let's begin with our young people. Boys, I have here a lovely pink and white box. I can't show you what's inside, but whoever tells the best joke will find out! Do any of you know a good joke?

"Hey, I got one," said Larry, hopping off the stage

"So do I!" said Jac.

Before I knew it, I was sitting on the stage alone. I didn't like sitting alone. Nor did I like being stared at by the Detroit Lakes church family. *A good joke. Did I know a good joke? . . . Yes, I did! I did know a good joke!*

"All right," said the emcee. "Our three contestants are ready. Andy, you're the youngest. Why don't you go first?"

"OK," I said. "What gets wetter and wetter the more it dries?" The joke was a sure winner—no one had ever answered it.

"A towel," replied a woman in the front row.

"Yeah, that's it," I said. A few people clapped politely (a bad sign).

Next was Larry. Larry told a joke about a boy who forgot his ABCs. The place roared. People went into convulsions. I was so distraught that I didn't even hear Jac's joke. Larry won in a landslide and quickly claimed the double-chocolate brownies that Jenny Rogers had made.

The emcee then had us, the two losers, compete for another box by playing basketball—the first one to make five shots would win. I sank four shots before Jac even made one. Then I froze, and Jac walked away with Valerie Nelson's fresh apple pie. Embarrassed, I escaped back to the stage.

Meanwhile, the men's competition had begun. The men came in three groups: single men, married men who competed only for their wives' desserts,[2] and married men who knew no such boundaries.[3] The highlight of this segment was a bidding war between Dad and Virgil Krogstad (both "no boundary" men) over an extravagant-looking basket brought by a woman named Arla. The basket itself wasn't the issue; pride was. Neither man could stand the thought of being outbid. The basket was finally sold to Virgil Krogstad at $100 even. The church was hysterical.

This is all very nice, I thought from my perch on the

2. "Wives only" men fell into three subgroups: 1) those so in love with their wives that they couldn't imagine eating dessert with anyone else, 2) those who didn't want other men eating dessert with their wives, and 3) those who had been warned against competing for other desserts—*or else.*

3. "No boundary" men fell into two subgroups: 1) those whose relationships were so secure that they could have competed for a dessert made by Farrah Fawcett and it wouldn't have mattered, and 2) those men who were tired of the same old dessert.

stage. *Everyone in this whole gym has a dessert, except me. That's fine. I'll just sit here and starve and watch everyone eat. I'll just—*

"Andy!" It was Mom. "Don't you have a dessert yet?" I slapped the air downward—code for "Leave me alone"—but off she went to tell the emcee.

"OK!" said the emcee. "It seems we have a couple fellas who don't have desserts. Pastor Bruce and Andy, come on up front! Take these brooms and pretend to ride horseback. Whoever does the best impression wins!"

Looking back, I know that the church meant well. I know that they gave me an easy game so I, too, would win something. I know that the emcee's saying "Come on, folks! Let's encourage him!" was intended to make me feel happy. But, as I galloped around the gym, clutching my broom-horse, I didn't feel happy. I felt dumb. *This isn't a real game,* I thought. *They're just letting me win.*

And as I sat there, having dessert with a nineteen-year-old named Susie who looked as distressed as I felt, I knew that we had something in common: For both of us, "box social" had been a night to forget.

Control

It's well-documented. Children who grow up Adventist in small traditional churches in small traditional towns are bound to have a few restless moments.[1] For me, nine of ten came during the 11 o'clock worship hour.

By the time my friends and I had reeled in our memory verse fish, exploded out of primary, dodged suitpants and skirts down the hall, and found our families in the sanctuary, we were wide-eyed and ready for action. About then the head elder invited us to turn to antiphonal reading number 804—again, that's number 804—where he would read the dark print, we the light, and it was hard not to get discouraged. Church just couldn't compete with Mom's Bible stories at home, and sometimes I wondered why everyone didn't just stay home and let their moms read to them.

Of course, the service always included a children's story—

---

1. Those children who never get restless are not normal and should be checked.

a fun five minutes except when the storyteller played to the grownups too much—but after that, what were we supposed to do? Read the *Review*?

Angel and I had heard rumors about churches down in Florida that offered *separate* children's services where kids enjoyed Bible games and Bible puppet shows and, just for a change of pace, went out into nature—God's second book—and petted rabbits and picked dandelions and learned so much about their world and then came back inside to hear short mission features about oppressed children in churches up north who were expected to keep still for sixty minutes straight, a little like Ezekiel, because families simply should not be split for the worship hour—or so it was believed there.

This belief, however, didn't change what we were—children. And, being children, we did what children needed to do in large quiet rooms—giggle.

Giggling in church was never planned. We knew that giggling was irreverent and besides, it hurt. Holding in a good giggle is hard,[2] especially when your sister is desperately trying to do the same thing. You feel her shake and you do everything to avoid looking at her because if you do, you're gone. Giggling is even worse than crying. Crying children can escape to the cry room; giggling children have no such refuge. You just sit hunched, head in hands, trying to convince yourself that that man's ridicu-

2. Just ask the charismatics in Toronto.

lously loud sneeze wasn't *that funny*, so just stop it! But then she begins to shake again.

Some mothers with giggling kids tried to cure them by providing Bible coloring books and stickers. My mom provided Sun-maid raisins. Raisins were the perfect snack—not bad for you like candy, yet not *too* healthful either. I was almost always in the mood for raisins and even when I wasn't, I ate them because when the box was empty, it could be made into a very realistic looking boat. "Look, Mom—Noah's Ark," I would whisper; she would smile. But before long, even raisins backfired.

Sitting four rows up and to the right were the Klein kids. Eric and Val Klein were several years older than us—too old for raisins. But each week Angel and I noticed the round faces of the Klein kids looking back at us longingly. *They were coveting our raisins.* We began to eat our raisins more deliberately now, slowly removing single morsels from our boxes and popping them into our mouths, chewing with delighted smiles—*my, these taste wonderful*—as we reached for more. This made the Klein kids *want* to start giggling, but they *couldn't* or they would get in trouble, all of which was very enjoyable to watch.

Meanwhile, unbeknownst to us, Dad had caught on to our little game. He wasn't pleased. It was one thing for his children to keep themselves entertained; it was quite another for them to interrupt other families. The line had been crossed. Dad prepared his forefinger. It was time for "The Tap."

To its recipient,[3] The Tap feels like a thick dowel being driven into the upper recesses of the shoulder. There, it lingers a moment—long enough to establish its presence—and then retreats, with an extra press for good measure. The Tap was a devastating blow to a delinquent child—not as painful as it was humbling. Never did The Tap fail to send its message: *You know better than that.*

And I did. I did know better than that. And I was sorry for shaming my family just so I could have a cheap laugh. *How selfish!*

"I'll do better next time, Dad," I said as we walked to the car, his hand resting on my shoulder.

"I know you will, pal," he said.

As I got older, I giggled less and enjoyed church more. And today, when I see children with glazed looks, I remember what they're going through, what questions they're asking: What *is* an antiphonal reading? How many knotholes *are* on that ceiling? Is that clock *broken*?

And when I see them giggling, head in hands, I'm glad when their parents harness the urge to roughly forbid them and, instead, discipline gently—enough to temper the giggling, but not the joy. Because the church's biggest asset is not simply children, but children with smiles on their faces. And I hope they stay there.

3. Me. I was older.

Potluck

On the surface, a church potluck may seem a relatively simple affair. Make something. Wrap it in aluminum foil. Bring it to church. Watch everyone eat it. Listen discreetly for reactions.

But more is involved. Much more.

From the preparer's standpoint, the church potluck doesn't begin on Sabbath at 12:05, though her husband may think it does.[1] It begins days—nay, weeks—beforehand. First, she must decide what type of food item to bring to church: a salad, a dessert, or a hot dish.[2] Variety is encouraged, lest she be thought one-dimensional. If she chooses the hot dish, she must decide at which point during the sermon she will

---

1. Reminder: Our setting here is the 1970s. Men hadn't been liberated yet.
2. "Hot dish" is Minnesotan for "casserole." We use it for a couple of reasons. First, "casserole" is a heavy word, demanding more syllables than it deserves. Second, "hot dish" gives us a chance to brush up on the word "hot." Most of the year we have no reason to use it.

slip down to the kitchen to make the dish hot—put another away, she decides how much she'll be fed spiritually before seeing that others get fed physically.

From a kid's standpoint, potlucks are no less complex. Initially, the looming questions are, *What kind of food will be served?* and *If a new kind of food is served, should I risk trying it?* Early on, I developed my own personal potluck philosophy: stick with what you know.

Once, as a little twerp, I had gone through the potluck line with my friends and they had said, "Cool! Tacos!" so I grabbed one. Back at the table, though, I wished I hadn't. Not knowing how to eat a taco, every time I tried to take a bite (out of the middle), the shell cracked a little bit more. My taco was quickly collapsing. Tomatoes, lettuce, and sour cream oozed onto my plate while my friends threw down their napkins and bolted off to the dessert bar. I wept.

Soon, Dad looked down the table and noticed his son sobbing over a taco. It couldn't have been one of his prouder days. Nevertheless, he came to my rescue. "Tacos are kind of tricky to eat, aren't they, pal?" he asked.

"Mm-hmm," I whimpered.

"But," he said, "*haystacks* are much easier."

"What do you mean?" I asked.

Taking a fork, Dad crushed my taco shell and spread the contents evenly around my plate. "There," he said. "Now you have a haystack, and no one else does."

Seconds later, I was enthusiastically scooping up my haystack—which no one else had—and hoping that someday I'd be as smart as Dad.

A bigger problem, though, than food that's hard to get into your mouth is food that's hard to eat once it's there. Few things match the confusion of shoveling in a spoonful of, say, something yellow (many potluck dishes are yellow) and then realizing it wasn't what you had expected. Perhaps it's cold and you thought it would be hot. Perhaps it carried a surprise in the middle.

That's why *sticking with what you know* is the best approach. Of course, one of the best ways to stick with what you know is to eat what Mom brought. Granted, playing it safe never won anyone a championship; there's always that chance you'll miss out on a dream dish—perhaps the combination of nutritious and delicious for which you've always searched. But by staying with Mom's food, you know your hunger will be satisfied and so will she.

By far, though, the biggest childhood concern at potluck is not *What will I get to eat?* but *When will I get to eat it?* Unlike other churches I'd visited, Detroit Lakes children weren't sent to the front of the line *en masse*; we waited until our families' table was called. After the blessing, Pastor Tim would start calling tables on one side of the room and systematically work his way to the other side.

Sometimes I'd try to get a good read on which side of the room Pastor Tim might begin with. I'd listen to his sermon for hints. One week, for example, he preached about "the sheep and the goats." The sheep, he said, were those on the right hand, while the goats were on the left. Clearly this was a sign that, to go first through that day's potluck line, you should sit on Pastor Tim's *right*. At my urging we did, and sure enough, he chose our table first—told ya so.

But my fortune wasn't always so good. One Sabbath, we sat on the far left side, a risky move. On one hand, we might be the very first table called. On the other, we might be the very—

Toomp toomp toomp. Pastor Tim was tapping the microphone.

"OK," he said, his eyes sparkling. "It's time to begin our fellowship dinner. If you happened to catch a glimpse of today's meal, you'll not want to wait a moment longer."

He was right; we *didn't* want to wait a moment longer. Pastor Tim looked over to our side; I smiled my best smile at him. Then he looked back to the other side. The tension was building. You could have cut it with a—

"Wes," he said, pointing at Wes Nelson clear on the other side of the room. "Why don't you and your table go through line first?"

I was thrown. Pastor Tim had really let me down. *Was it something I said?* I didn't have time to figure it out. I had to salvage what I could.

It was too late to join the Nelson table. That would look obvious. But at the next table over sat the Umbers. I hadn't visited with the Umbers in a while. Perhaps now would be a good time to catch up.

"I'm going to go sit by the Umbers," I said to Mom.

"No, you're not," she said, laughing. "You stay right here with us."

It would be another 30 minutes before our table was called. I passed the time by resenting all the people who were going through line ahead of me. There they were—smiling, laughing, taking their sweet time. *Oh, never mind our table*, I thought. *We're happy to just sit here and watch you pile your plates high. No hurry at all. . . . Oh, did you forget your drink, sir? Well, by all means, go ahead and jump back in line. We'll wait. We have all afternoon—assuming we don't starve to death first.*

By the time we shuffled through line, only remnants of a once-respectable selection remained. The au gratin potato pan had been scraped clean. Small slabs of orange Jello drooped over the edges of a plate. Two green beans huddled in the corner of a large pot. A corn muffin sat alone, cold and hard. Worst of all, almost every dish carried traces of cucumber salad. Apparently, some kid had used the same spoon all the way through line.

From that day on, we sat smack dab in the middle. It seemed to be the safest option. Sure, you might have to wait a few extra minutes to eat, meaning that by dessert time, the chocolate brownies might be gone. But you had peace of mind that way, allowing you to focus on your conversation with those around you—your Adventist family.

Normally, of course, potlucks were attended only by Adventists. But one memorable Sabbath, a visiting non-Adventist family decided to hang around for the fellowship dinner the bulletin had invited them to. Wanting to contribute to the feast but not aware of the Adventist vegetarian lifestyle, the family rushed to the parking lot after church, got in their car, and made a quick trip to the local Kentucky Fried Chicken. Returning with a giant bucket of drumsticks, the couple proudly placed their contribution in the food line and then watched bewilderedly as church member after church member approached the chicken, paused,[3] and then moved on to the Special K loaf.

Noticing that no one had partaken of the visitors' food offering, Pastor Tim sauntered over to the potluck line, grabbed a plate, reached into the bucket, and retrieved a nice fat drumstick. For a moment, silence fell over the fellowship hall, not unlike the silence just before an avalanche. Then, as though in tandem, the seated "vegetarians" broke for the chicken.

I watched the stampede from the dessert bar. By the time I worked my way back to my table, they were coming so fast that I worried about my safety—and that of my chocolate fudge brownie. In a scramble to get out of their way, I nearly dropped it on the fellowship hall's new carpet. That, of course, would have been disastrous. All they had left was carob cookies.

3. Some members paused longer than others.

Persecuted

I had hoped that my flight wouldn't come in the winter, but a cold winter wind was slapping my face and a foot of snow was tugging at my boots. I trudged up Indian Hill and into the woods. My eyes darted from tree to tree. And my heart raced.

Blessed are the persecuted, I kept telling myself. *Blessed are the persecuted.*

No sign of the wicked, but I couldn't be too sure. The Time of Trouble was here, and I was fleeing deep into the woods with only my Bible and cornbread rations.

Suddenly, three figures came bolting down a broad path from the opposite direction. I dove behind a dead bush, sure that they would see me through the bare branches. But they ran right by. My relief lasted only a second. I watched the persecutors veer left off the path and hone in on a small boulder.

"Oh, no!" cried a voice. "Please don't take me!" *That voice,* I thought. *That voi—*

Micky! I recognized the screams of my friend and fellow Sabbath keeper. What was *she* doing here? "Please don't take me!"

I had to decide fast. I decided. "I'm coming, Mick! I'm coming!"

The persecutors whirled around to see what kind of fool Sabbath keeper had disclosed himself. As I approached, the big one in the middle, the one they called Erki, recognized me. "I've been looking for you, Nash!" he bellowed. "I've been looking for you for a *long* time!"

"Let's get him!" hollered the persecutors.

Glad to divert their attention from the helpless Micky, I spun around and began to weave through the trees in an elaborate pattern. (My dad had shown me this technique years before.) My weaving was working well until two more persecutors leaped out from behind a boulder and tackled me. One grabbed my arms and held them behind my back as the other punched my stomach. To my astonishment, I realized the one punching me was a former Adventist.

"Why, Todd?" I said between blows. "Why are you doing this? We used to be friends. Remember, Todd? *Friends!*"

Todd nodded slowly and exhaled. "Yes, Andy, we used to be friends," he said. "But things are different now. You see, the gover—" Todd stopped. A whistle was blowing in the distance.

No, not the whistle, I thought. Anything but that. "No, not now," moaned Todd. "We just got here."

"Kii-iids! Kii-iids! Come on, kids! Recess is ooovvvverr! It was our church school teacher, Mr. Rogers. We hung our heads and began to walk back. The Time of Trouble would have to wait until tomorrow.

Persecution. I thought about it a lot as a child. I think a lot of Adventist children do. Baptist children hear about hellfire; we hear about persecution. In Sabbath School I learned about Stephen and the other early Christians, and how someday we, too, will be persecuted for our beliefs.

In fourth grade, we read *The Persecutor*, the story of a Russian named Sergei Kordakov who persecuted the "believers." Sergei Kordakov would break into secret prayer meetings and beat the believers ruthlessly. Once he clubbed a girl again and again because she wouldn't cry, and she bit through her bottom lip. Later, Sergei Kordakov became a believer himself and escaped by jumping off a Russian ship into Canadian waters. But the Russians found and killed him too. *The Persecutor* inspired us to play The Time of Trouble in the woods at recess. Half of us were the persecutors; half were the persecuted. But that was all just pretend.

The only thing close to real persecution I knew of was when my parents were unfair to me. Like the time Dad brought a big pink and yellow piñata to a church social and let all the other kids, even the big kids, have a whack at it before I could. By the time they were blindfolding sixteen-year-old Bobby, I, a seven-year-old, was devastated. Bobby smashed the piñata and the other kids scrambled for the candy, but I didn't want any. All I had wanted was a chance to hit the piñata and be a hero.

Mom persecuted me too. As my church school teacher, she never *ever* let me have the good classroom jobs, like cleaning the blackboard or handing back papers. I always got stuck with washing the sink or vacuuming. Finally, one day, with tears in my eyes, I grabbed her hand, dragged her out to the hallway, and said, "Mrs. Nash, why are you meaner to me than to all the other kids?" Then she started to cry, too, and I figured she felt bad for persecuting me.

Still, I knew this wasn't even close to what Sergei Kordakov's victims had to go through. I had never bitten through my lip to keep from crying. I had never watched wicked people take my family away. I didn't have any idea what real persecution was like, and I was terrified about some-day finding out.

And so I thought about persecution a lot. Especially in bed at night. I knew what we were supposed to do when it came. And I knew we weren't supposed to be afraid when it did. But I *was* afraid. I couldn't help being afraid. Persecution was a scary word.

Juniors

Not unlike the many stages of life are the many stages of Sabbath School. Each stage holds its own charm. Yet one stage noses ahead of the pack, declaring itself the essence of Sabbath School—Juniors.

Why juniors? Because in cradle roll through kindergarten, you're cute but you're clueless. You instinctively swing your little left arm during "Father Abraham," but you have no idea what it means. In teens and youth, you know what things mean, but you don't participate—you're too cool. And in adults, your discussion is mature but abstract, a perpetual debate over faith and works.

Only juniors offers the perfect blend of fun and growth, of innocence and cognizance. At least it did where I grew up.

Juniors begins with song service. We use the *Advent Youth Sing*. Whenever my mom plays the piano, we call out number 178, "The Captain Calls," because we love her reaction—disgust. "Not this song again," she says, laughing, and then she hammers out the chords while we sing of the mighty task to do . . . "Volunteers! Volunteers! Vol-un-teers!"

That out of the way, we go through our usual repertoire—"A Quiet Place" (no. 2), "Pass It On" (152), "Love Was When" (28), and "In My Heart There Rings a Melody" (95). Inevitably, someone calls out "number 215," and several people flip to the back of the songbook because they've forgotten: There *isn't* any 215. Everyone chuckles.

Then someone calls out "166" and we don't even turn to it. Everyone knows 166 is "Side by Side." The piano leads in with "pray that we'll all be there," and we sing loudly, enjoying the familiarity, hoping that no one will confuse "join hands together" with "sing songs together," reveling in the idea that "we'll fight in faith and we will overcome."

"OK," says the teacher. "It's time for the mission story." We look around to see which junior has it this week.

It's quiet for several seconds until finally Ruth Umber says, "Oh, all right," and drags up front. "I haven't even read it," she says, which builds our anticipation even more. Big foreign names, here she comes.

Ruth's a good reader, though, and doesn't goof as much as we had hoped. The story's about a man named Raul who does great things in Costa Rica.[1]

The teacher then pulls out a checklist to see what great things *we* did this past week, a mini-investigative judgment.

---

1. The reward for reading the mission story up front is that you get to pass it on to whomever you choose. It's a dramatic moment. No one's making eye contact; all heads are bowed. Then you say it. "Danny?"

"Persons helped," she says. "Let's start with Larry Burgeson . . ."

Good. I have time. I think hard: *Who did I help? I did the dishes—that helped Mom. I stacked firewood—that helped Dad. Actually, that helped all of us. Helped keep us warm. And there must be others I haven't thought of.*

"Andy? How many?

"Nine," I say humbly, knowing that my deeds pale next to Raul's. . . . *yeah, but they're just as good Larry's.* I don't have much time to rationalize. We're onto the next category: literature distributed.

After a couple exciting rounds of Bible password[2], we begin the lesson study. Samson's an intriguing guy, but I'm distracted by the *Guide*, which I picked up earlier. I scour the list of pen pals, looking for people with hobbies that match mine: sports, reading, making friends. I keep forgetting to send mine in.[3]

"Andy, what do *you* think about the Philistines?"

I don't know what to say. I've been reading the *Guide*.

Luckily, I'm rescued by Don Strom, who pops in his head and holds up two fingers—two minutes left.

"OK," says the teacher, "we need to wrap up. Don't for-

---

2. Bible password is pretty much the same as regular password, except that we use Bible words such as "flood," "vine," and "tax collector."
3. My sister got hers published. It read: Angel Nash; animals, piano, gymnastics; P.O. Box 479; Detroit Lakes, Minnesota. A couple months later she got a letter from a boy in Kenya. The address on the envelope read: Angel Nash; animals, piano, gymnastics; P.O. Box 479; Detroit Lakes, Minnesota.

get about the canoeing trip next Sunday." She closes with prayer, and we scramble down the hall past the adult room where someone is insisting that "faith without works is dead." I recognize the voice. It's the same guy who declined the invitation to help with Juniors this quarter.

It's too bad really. He doesn't know what he's missing.

Door to Door

Adventist kids and girl scouts have a lot in common. Like girl scouts, Adventist kids spend much of their childhood—in some cases, up to half—going door to door. But unlike girl scouts, Adventist kids don't go door to door for the purpose of selling something that crumbles easily at a special rate of six dollars—how many boxes would you like? No, Adventist kids don't use such gimmicks; they just flat out ask for something.

When I was a kid, we asked for two things: money and food. Surprisingly, collecting money, or "ingathering," had limited appeal. Certainly it's always pleasant to see your can stuffed with cash.[1] But many people didn't give cash; they

---

1. The first cash donation was made by a fellow church member using a technique called "seeding," in which a couple crisp bills are placed in such a way as to peek out the top of the can, enticing the solicitee to think that his neighbor had made a donation, so he had better do the same. As far as I know, "seeding" was the only time it was OK to bear false witness.

wrote checks, and it got dull waiting for a guy to find his pen and checkbook—now who should I make that out to?

By far the most exciting item to collect was canned goods for the poor and needy. Somehow, in this venue, food held a new attraction. The same vegetables that were boring to eat at last night's supper suddenly took on an aura of excitement. *Oooh, a can of corn. Oooh, asparagus.*

We, the church school, collected cans around Halloween time.[2] Before we hit the streets, though, Mr. Rogers and Mrs. Nash assembled us downstairs in the fellowship hall to go over some "ground rules." Mr. Rogers reminded us not to comment on the type of canned goods we received. If someone gave us pork and beans, just accept it graciously and remember to say thanks.

If we get pork, will we give it to the poor? someone had to ask.

Yes, we will, he would answer. The poor needed food, not a health lecture.

Then they broke us into pairs and gave us our street assignments. Jac and I were assigned to West Lake Drive— exactly what I had hoped for. For weeks, on the bus ride home, I had been eyeing a huge stone house on West Lake Drive, a can collector's dream. Such a beautiful home was sure to produce more cans than we could even carry. Perhaps the owners would have their servants load the cans into their private limo parked around back, just out of sight,

---

2. The timing suited us just fine—yes, of course we'll accept your candy as a token of appreciation for our efforts.

and drive to the church with Jac and I in the back seat sipping ginger ale and watching cable. The *Detroit Lakes Tribune* would probably want to feature us on page one. "Can Collectors Strike Gold, World Hunger Ended."

Our anticipation growing, Jac and I climbed the steep driveway, pushed the doorbell dramatically, and rocked back and forth on our feet until a small white-haired lady opened it.

"Hello, boys," she said, sweetly.

"Hi," I said. "My name's Andy and this is Jac. We're from the Seventh-day Adventist Church School and we're collecting cans for the poor and needy."

"What?" she said. "Cans?"

"Yes—for the poor and needy."

"OK . . . just one minute, please."

She closed the door a little to keep the draft out and walked away. Jac and I looked at each other. This was it—our big break. The limo should be warming up behind the house any time now. The servants should be on their way.

The door swung open, and there they were—the woman and a tiny can of peas. "Here you go, boys," she said. "Bye now."

My biggest regret as I walked back down the hill was not that the huge stone house hadn't yielded the bountiful harvest I'd expected but that I had told all the other kids it would. *Maybe they've forgotten*, I reasoned. They hadn't.

"So what'd you get from the huge stone house?" they asked in the van.

"A can of peas."

"A can of peas? That's *it?*"

Back at school, they had finally stopped convulsing and messing up my hair. I smoothed it down while Mr. Rogers emptied our morning's work onto three long potluck tables. My tiny can of peas rolled in with dozens of other more prestigious-looking cans, including a whole gallon of pears, but Mr. Rogers declared it didn't matter who collected what. All that mattered, he said, his voice building, was that a few more area families would go to bed tonight with full stomachs and smiles on their faces because of the good work we had done for mankind, and we should all be very, very proud.

Baptism

I got baptized with three girls when I was nine. My original plan was to get baptized with three boys when I was eight. But Larry, Jac, and Danny each had a couple years on me, so my parents and pastor suggested I wait for the next batch of candidates—Micky, Rocky, and Jenny. I would be more "ready" then, they said.

I never quite understood what everyone meant when they talked about my being "ready" for baptism. I knew it didn't mean the physical act of being baptized itself—granted, I wasn't known for my swimming prowess,[1] but I could certainly handle being underwater for a few seconds. I figured that being "ready" meant knowing stuff: which day was the Sabbath (Saturday), what you shouldn't do on Sabbath (bring your electronic football game to church), what happened when you died (noth-

---

1. At swimming lessons, I was the coughing, flailing kid all the other kids waited for at the edge of the pool. "Somebody throw him a kickboard," said the teacher, the ultimate disgrace.

ing), and how long hell will last (not long).

Only during baptismal studies did I learn that being "ready" meant, as Pastor Heglund put it, "accepting Jesus Christ as your personal Lord and Saviour."

That sounded simple enough. I loved Jesus. I particularly loved how He treated others—the children on His lap, Zaccheus in the tree, the blind man on the side of the road.[2] Jesus seemed to specialize in giving people a break—a good lesson for all to follow (even if your kid should accidentally bring his electronic football game to church). As loving and kind as Jesus was, why *wouldn't* I accept Him as my "personal Lord and Saviour"?

But as I studied more about Jesus' life and mission, I began to wonder whether I really understood enough about Him to be considered "ready." Especially confusing was the part about Jesus dying on a cross for our sins. I knew the event was important, but I had trouble connecting with it. The empty tomb? *That* I could connect with—no one expected Jesus to walk out of there but He did, the greatest comeback in history.

But the Cross and the priestly ministry and the cleansing of the heavenly sanctuary—if I didn't understand all the things a Saviour did, was I allowed to accept Jesus as my "Lord and Saviour?" Would people even believe that I loved Him?

The day of our baptism, the girls and I sang "He's My Friend" up front,[3] separated to change into our gowns, and reunited at

2. "The very first thing he saw," read Arthur Maxwell's *Bible Story* book, "was the face of Jesus smiling upon him." My sister and I knew the story by heart.
3. The second time through, Micky, Jenny, and I each had a solo line. Mine was "My heart sings with the joy of His love and fav-or."

the baptismal tank, where suddenly it was my turn.

"And so, "said Pastor Heglund, "because of your decision to follow Jesus, I now baptize you . . ." My hands clenched his wrist. ". . . in the name of the Father . . ." My heart pounded. ". . . and of the Son. . ." My breath stopped. ". . . and of the Holy Spirit . . ." My heels lifted. "Amen."

Liquid peace engulfed, then streamed down, my face as Pastor Heglund dipped me in the water and then posed with me for a picture.

Dad, who took the picture, had watched my public decision in private—in the quiet shadows just off-stage, where he was most comfortable. Afterward, he walked me down to the junior room so I could change. On the chair, beside my brown corduroy suit, was a hairdryer.

"What's that for?" I asked.

"Oh, you don't want to go back upstairs with your hair all wet, do you?" he said.

I hadn't really thought about it.

Dad dried my hair while I dressed, and we didn't say much. The hair dryer was too loud for talking, anyway. But as he switched to low speed and then quit drying altogether, it seemed as though he wanted to tell me something but didn't know how.

He unplugged the hair dryer, wound it up, and set it down.

"Ready to go?" I asked.

He cupped my head and pulled me into his chest. "I'm glad you love Jesus, pal," he said.

It was just what I needed to hear.

Public School

Christian homes are different from other homes. Christian homes keep the Sabbath on Saturday. Other homes go to church on Sunday or don't go to church at all. Christian people are kind. Other homes are kind only some of the time. Christians don't watch TV on the Sabbath. Other homes do. Even if other homes have different ways, I still like them.—Andy Nash, 8

The summer before fifth grade, I prepared for a dramatic change in my life—a transfer from church school to public school. The reason? There were no boys left in church school. They all had either graduated or moved. A new wave was rolling in, the wave being led by my sister and her friends, none of whom respected me, their elder, as they should. To a purist, an eleven-to-one girl/boy ratio might not seem like reason enough to leave the Adventist school system. To a ten-year-old, it was plenty of reason. My parents agreed.

Technically, I had already attended public school for two years—kindergarten and first grade—but when you're that young, you don't think a whole lot about the type of school you're attending. My early school days were built around playing marbles at recess, "happy notes" from the teacher, and walking to my grandma's house after school to eat frosted blueberry Pop-Tarts and watch *Gilligan's Island.* I remember very little from class time itself, except that Amy Hesby twisted my arm practically every time the teacher looked away and that I was the first one in the whole class to correctly read the word "pigeon."[1]

That's about it. No recollection of first graders in the hallway pulling me aside offering me drugs or of teachers seducing me into the New Age. When you're that young, school is just school. The only barometer of those around you is whether they're nice and how fast they can run, the latter being the most important.

By fifth grade, though, it's different. I had had plenty of exposure to Adventism's distinctive beliefs, plenty of opportunities to see that we were a "peculiar people"—or at least that we were supposed to be. If it wasn't a great gulf that I saw fixed between Adventists and the rest of the world, it was at least a mighty river. I was now well aware of the three angels' messages (a prophetic calling that we seemed to own),

---

1. Mrs. Johnston gave our reading group a new word and told us it was a type of bird. But "pigeon" was a trick word. Up until that week, "g" always made a hard sound, as in the word "gag." We went around the circle and kids guessed "penguin" and "parrot" and "pig on" (which made no sense but made all of us laugh). Then, suddenly, I remembered the new "soft g" rule—a bolt of wisdom from above. "Pigeon," I said. "That's right," said Mrs. Johnston. Everyone was astounded.

the tension between Adventists and Catholics, and the world's most dangerous man, the pope.

I had first heard of the pope a couple summers earlier at the community recreation center ("the rec") downtown. Between at bats in t-ball, my friend Chris Fossen was talking about someone called the pope. I remember thinking that it was such a strange word. "Who's the pope?" I asked Chris. Baffled at my ignorance, he explained that the pope was in charge of all the churches around the world.

"I don't think he's in charge of my church," I said.

"Oh yes he is," said Chris. "He's in charge of all of them."

I'm not sure why the idea of one man being in charge of all the world's churches didn't sound right to me. I'd like to think it was because I knew enough about Jesus to understand that we didn't need anyone else, but I can't say for sure that this was the reason. Maybe I just didn't like the word *pope*.

By fifth grade, though, I had developed a rather clear opinion of the pope. He was bad news. Oh, sure, he might ride around in his glassed-in Popemobile waving at the crowds and blessing little children, but deep down he was thinking one thing and one thing only: Sunday laws.

The terrible thought of Sunday laws—and the persecution that would come with them—led me to leeriness over anything or *anyone* associated with them. It wasn't that I saw Sunday keepers as evil. I knew people could go to church on Sunday and still be nice. But neither could I see Sunday keepers as being legitimate Christians. After all, if Sunday keeping was so wrong, so unbiblical, how could anyone who went to church on Sunday be good enough to be called a Christian? It just didn't add up.[2]

So this was the baggage I brought with me back to public school. While I hoped to enjoy myself there, I knew that I would always need to keep a little distance, lest I become part of the world. After all, I was different.

A few weeks before school began, however, I encountered something that jarred the neat little dichotomy I had set up—a friend.

Jim Wood and I met at registration for summer saxophone lessons. I hadn't planned to choose the saxophone; I wanted to play the trumpet. But when I got to the sign-up table, they already had too many trumpets, so they asked whether I'd take the saxophone instead. I looked at Dad; I hadn't expected to face such a major decision. "You'll like the saxophone too," he said, so I signed up.

By this time, Mom was talking to a woman over by the door. A boy about my age stood beside them holding a pink piece of paper. Apparently, he had already been through the sign-up line.

"Andy, come here," mouthed Mom.

---

2. Sometimes our church tried to share our distinctive beliefs through evangelistic series, which were held sporadically—whenever an evangelist came to town. The first few sessions always went well. We mixed with our non-Adventist friends, received free Bibles for bringing five of them at one time, and sang "He Lives" every night—boy, Barb Halvorsen sure could hit those high notes. But, invariably, when the evangelist got to the Sabbath doctrine, attendance would drop off dramatically. Little boastful horns or not, they weren't going to change their whole lives now.

"No," I mouthed back. I didn't like the pressure of having to meet someone.

"Come *here*," she said, her forefinger jabbing down in perfect sync with her words.

Moments later, I was saying Hi to Nancy Wood and her son Jim who had also signed up for the saxophone. Oh, isn't that neat? said our moms. You two can take lessons together and become buddies.

Normally such a buildup was a bad omen, an arranged marriage destined to fail miserably. But I liked Jim from the start. He smiled a lot and seemed quite comfortable talking with my mom. I wondered, though, whether he would accept me. Jim seemed to be on a higher level of "cool" than I was. He dressed cool, and his blond hair was feathered back and parted in the middle. My hair had never seen a part in its life. It flopped down from a double crown[3] the same way it always had, a bowlcut from birth.

Jim didn't seem to care that I wasn't as cool as him. He came in and sat next to me at our saxophone lesson the next Wednesday morning, and by the time it was over, we were both so equally grossed out that we had bonded.

Our teacher, Mr. Sletto, began the lesson by telling us that the saxophone can't simply be pulled out of its case and played as, for example, a trumpet could.

---

3. A double crown can also be called a double cowlick. But I didn't like the way "double cowlick" sounded, so at the beauty shop (another term I didn't like, but that's where Mom took me), I warned the lady not to cut my "double crown" too short. If you're going to have a clump of hair sticking up all your life, you might as well give it a dignified name.

Great, I thought. *I knew I should have chosen the trumpet.*

Instead, Mr. Sletto pulled out a small thin piece of wood, which he called a "reed," and told us how the reed must be damp in order for the saxophone to play. "Put the reed in your mouth and suck on it," said Mr. Sletto, so we did.

After we had sucked on our reeds for a while, Mr. Sletto showed us how to fasten them onto our mouthpieces. "OK," he said, "go ahead and try to get a sound out of your instruments."

As we took enormous breaths and honked away on notes that only a parent could love (but often didn't), I noticed that Jim wasn't getting any sound from his saxophone. He kept blowing and blowing, but nothing came out. Observing the problem, Mr. Sletto went over to Jim and said, "Here, let me see that a minute." Unfastening the reed from the mouthpiece, Mr. Sletto said, "Your reed must not be damp enough." Then he did the unthinkable—*he put the reed in his mouth.*

"You thee," slurped Mr. Sletto. "You gothu thuck on the reed tho you can play your thaxaphone."

After a couple minutes of contamination, Mr. Sletto removed the reed, refastened it, blew a couple notes, and handed the saxophone back to Jim.

"Now try it," he said.

Jim examined the mouthpiece. It practically dripped with Mr. Sletto's saliva. "Go ahead," urged Mr. Sletto. Jim looked over at me; I shrugged my shoulders. Finally Jim eased the mouthpiece into his mouth and blew a big flat C-sharp, the note that comes out when you don't know which keys to press.

Satisfied, Mr. Sletto turned to see if anyone else needed assistance. "Andy, how's yours working?" he asked.

"Oh, just fine," I said quickly. "It's working just fine."

Afterward, Jim and I laughed all the way to our moms' cars. (I laughed a little louder than Jim did.) I reminded him that he probably never would get *all* of Mr. Sletto's spit out of his saxophone, he punched me in the shoulder, and our friendship was cemented.

By the end of summer saxophone lessons and a half dozen afternoons of water skiing, Jim and I had become best friends. We were thrilled to learn that we would both be in the same classroom, number 109, at Rossman Elementary. "Mr. Burgeson's going to be the coolest teacher," I said. "I know him."

Mr. Burgeson, of course, was from our church. My family had gotten together with the Burgeson family most every Saturday night for years. Mr. Burgeson had always been fun to go ice skating and play Uno with, so I reasoned that he'd probably be a fun teacher too. Sure enough—he was.

Mr. Burgeson read us hilarious books like *Me and Caleb*, helped us turn Styrofoam balls into giant revolving solar systems, and didn't even get angry when someone (I'm not saying who) wrote "Jim loves Stephanie!" in huge letters on the chalkboard before class.[4]

But Mr. Burgeson filled his classroom with more than

---

4. Actually, I was the one who loved Stephanie, but lacking the coolness and confidence to express my true feelings for her, I had to settle for loving her vicariously through Jim.

fun; he filled it with Christian principles—honesty, acceptance, awareness. He led us in daily discussions about current events because, he said, it was good for us to have a "little knowledge" about our world. Jim got elected president of our news sessions, which meant that he got to call on people and see what news they had to contribute. I got elected vice-president, which meant that if Jim were shot or if his school bus arrived late, I would need to be ready at a moment's notice.

Once, for science, Mr. Burgeson even showed us how silly evolution was. He began by taking the side of the evolutionist, telling us stories about slow-forming amoebae, which eventually turned into fish, which eventually turned into lizards, which eventually turned into monkeys, which eventually turned into humans—and then he finally stopped and asked us, "Do you believe these stories?" One kid in the back corner, Kevin Schooler, said that yes, he did believe these stories, but most of us just shook our heads. We weren't morons.

"You're going to hear a lot of strange ideas like this over the next several years," Mr. Burgeson told us. "People are going to tell you how life has been around for millions and millions of years and how we evolved from nothing. But you kids are smart enough to know that life doesn't just start from nothing. Don't let anyone tell you otherwise."

If fifth grade with Mr. Burgeson taught me to use my mind, sixth grade with Mr. Bucholz taught me to control it. Mr. Bucholz (pronounced "buckles") also coached the junior high football team, which automatically made him cool to me. But what impressed parents about Mr. Bucholz was his reputation for fair play. Dad called him a "class act." If there was one thing Mr. Bucholz wouldn't put up with, it was a poor sport—whether it be on his football team or in his classroom. When the weather was nice, Mr. Bucholz joined us outside for recess; one day he'd play football with the boys and Jennifer Marxen, the next day he'd play four square with the girls. Mr. Bucholz played to win and he often did. But when he didn't win, you wouldn't know the difference. He always smiled and said "good game," and he expected nothing less of us.

Indoors, however, was a game that Mr. Bucholz never lost at—chess. In fact, he hadn't been beaten in five years. All year my friends and I took turns losing to him. Losing to him almost became a game in itself:

"Play Mr. Bucholz today?"

"Yup."

"How long did you last?"

"Eight minutes."

"Eight minutes? Not bad."

Yet, one lunch hour in March, I somehow managed to take his queen early in the game, and from there it was just a matter of sustaining his furious challenge. A crowd of sixth graders had gathered around the board, and by the time I saw the winning move, I didn't even want to make it. No one likes to see a legend toppled, not even the one who's doing the toppling. But if I didn't make the move, I would be toying with the king, the worst crime of all. I knew he would want me to make it. So I did. "Checkmate," I said quietly, releasing my bishop. He kept his eyes on the board for a moment, just long enough to make sure there was no way out. Then he looked up at me, nodded once, and cleared his throat. "OK, class," he said, "Let's get out our history books." I never felt so terrible.

With teachers like Mr. Burgeson and Mr. Bucholz showing us how to handle the world in which God had put us, public school was a positive experience. That, of course, surprised me. I didn't expect to enjoy public school so much. Occasionally something, such as sausage pizza in the cafe or a school activity on Friday night, would fly in the face of my Adventist beliefs. But, for the most part, my religion went hand in hand with my schooling.

All that changed in junior high. Almost overnight, teachers weren't the heroes anymore. Bitterly competitive sports, pressure-packed school dances, who was gonna "get it" after school, beer kegs at our formerly tame get-togethers—these were the new heroes. Keeping up with news headlines? No one cared. Acceptance of those who dressed a little different? Forget it. God? A good word to use when something ticked you off.

By ninth grade, I was tired of my life and more insecure than ever. I'd come home after school, throw a blueberry Pop-Tart in the toaster, pour a glass of milk, and wonder if maybe it wasn't time to be different again.

Life

Once in school, I read that every nine seconds someone is born and that every fifteen seconds someone dies. These figures fascinated me, especially the death one. I knew what happened when we entered the world, but I had some concerns about the leaving part—namely, whether I'd be able to handle it if anyone ever left me.

Growing up, I never had a family member or close friend die. Several distant relatives and acquaintances died, but none were so dear to me that I really felt the hurt. The hot, bitter tears that streaked so many of my friends' faces never streaked mine.

And that was scary. I wasn't sure how I'd handle the death of someone I loved. I'd lie in bed at night and think about losing my little sister Angel, sleeping just down the hall. What if the house caught on fire and I jumped from my second-story window into a snowbank and Angel stood at her window too afraid to jump while I stood there helpless? How would I deal with that? What if my sorrow turned me against God and kept me out of heaven? Would the universe really go on and on and on without me?

Then my thoughts would drift from eternity-future to eternity-past. If time and God went back forever, I'd reason, how did we ever get to now? It blew my mind.

Even worse was the occasional fear that maybe God didn't exist at all. That, of course, was what atheists believed: We're only here because some little squiggly thing poked its head through the ground one afternoon and, like, three billion years later leapt into a lake and started swimming. I couldn't imagine being an atheist. Right or wrong, they were doomed. How could they sleep? How could they smile?

Then, wondering how I'd gotten onto the subject of whether atheists smile, I'd work my way back to my original concern—the pain of losing someone I loved, a pain I'd never known. Until I got my gun.

Hunting season. It was one of the few times I wished I didn't live in Minnesota, a sportsman's paradise. Hunting was part of our culture; public schools even made special allowances in their schedules for "opening day." Bus ride chatter turned from who would win this Sunday's game to who was going to shoot a twelve-point buck. Anyone who objected was promptly reminded that the deer population had to be thinned out, anyway, so go sit somewhere else if you can't handle it.

While shooting a deer never interested me (a lifelong *Bambi* fan), shooting a gun gradually gained appeal. So one spring I got one—a Daisy Red Rider—and a pack of BBs.

I started simply enough, pinging pop cans in our backyard. Soon, though, I found myself taking aim at targets that moved—sparrows, dragonflies, squirrels, all of which were hardly in danger. My BB gun was incredibly weak. I could click the trigger, unfold a blanket, sit down, and have a sandwich before the BB completed its pathetic arc. My "prey" always had plenty of time to escape. *Always*. I counted on it.

One afternoon Angel and I were walking alongside our lake, and a robin spun around an evergreen and took a seat. I casually raised my Daisy and clicked the trigger, causing the robin to hop off the branch and fly away. Except that it wasn't flying away; it was plunging like a pine cone twenty feet in front of us.

"You killed it!" screamed Angel, as we raced toward the bird that I hadn't quite killed. "It's bleeding!" she said.

Instinctively, I placed the barrel of my gun inches from the wounded bird and squeezed my eyes shut. "No!" she screamed. "I want to take it home!"

"I have to, Angel! It's suffering!"

She was halfway to the house by the time I sent three BBs into its orange breast. That night in bed the tears came, hot and bitter. I hadn't lost a loved one, but I'd severed the song of a cheerful little life. My family had forgiven me, and I'd promised never to shoot another animal *ever, ever again*. But that didn't bring the robin back.

Death, in all its cruelty, drove me deep into my pillow. And life, eternal life— where the tears would be wiped once and for all—never looked better.

Sabbath Afternoon Drives

Though it lost some steam during the gas shortages of the late '70s, the Sabbath afternoon drive chugs along as one of Adventism's most popular after-church activities.[1] Each Sabbath afternoon, following dinner, whole Adventist families (no matter how big) pile into their cars (no matter how small) to "go for a little drive in the country."

No one, of course, is sure *why* they have to go for a little drive in the country because no one really enjoys it much, except possibly Dad, who doesn't have to share his seat with anyone. But off they go, at about 1:30 or 2:00, to quibble over how much the window should be rolled down and who's going to hold the dog. They go out of habit, because those

---

1. It's second only to the Sabbath afternoon nap and its sister activity, the Sabbath afternoon sneak on your stomach and elbows into Mom and Dad's room without waking them. (Tip: If you start giggling while you're still on Mom's side of the bed, a little mercy might be shown, but if you get all the way around to Dad's side and *then* explode, it's all over.)

before them went—by '57 Chevy, by Model T, by horse and carriage,[2] all of which were much more exciting than a Subaru, but that's beside the point. Tradition is tradition.

There have been, however, a few Adventist families along the way that have taken some liberties with this tradition. It's not the going somewhere that they question; no one doubts that Adventists should go *somewhere* on Sabbath afternoon.[3] Rather, it's whether they have to go by *car*. For these Adventists, a ride in the car may present any of the following problems: (1) perpetual back-seat argument over whether someone's "line" had been crossed, (2) carsickness, or (3) November through April blizzards that make it hard to find the car, let alone the road.

Since my family often fell firmly in all of the above, we forsook the standard Sabbath afternoon drive in the car (and also the alternative Sabbath afternoon horseback ride after Mom's saddle slid under her horse), and we bought four red Honda three-wheelers instead.

That pretty much changed everything. Suddenly, Angel and I no longer dreaded, but anticipated, Sabbath afternoon drives. No longer would we have to sit and make faces at each other in the back seat of the car; now we could make faces at each other from our own vehicles.

Angel's vehicle was a Honda 70, which had three gears and was quicker than you might expect. She plastered an "Angela" sticker on its rear fender, in case anyone (me) might

---

2. "Hook up the team, Hiram. I'll get the sandwiches."
3. Again, the countryside is preferred. Fewer temptations.

have the notion to borrow it—as if I'd even want to. Mom
and I had 110s, which did the job. Dad drove a 175. He
needed a 175 (he told us) to make a good trail through the
three, sometimes fourteen, feet of snow that fell in Minnesota.

And so, after dinner each Sabbath, the four of us bundle
up in our long johns, snowpants, three pairs of wool socks,
moon boots, down-filled coats, scarves, neckwarmers, and
stocking caps. The process takes about twenty minutes—
just enough time for Angel to decide that, yes, she really
does have to go to the bathroom.

A half hour later, we're off—Dad in the lead, then Angel, then me, then, a few minutes later, Mom. Veering off
our icy driveway, Dad—rocking wildly left and right—plows
a jagged path through our snow-cloaked fields. He takes us
alongside the creek, which is mostly frozen but "never safe
to walk on," and towards the woods. As we stop and wait
for Mom to catch up,[4] Dad points at a white-tailed doe and
fawn, still as statues, about a hundred yards away. They're
looking right at us. Our staredown with the deer is spoiled
by the lone yap of our dog Casey, who has been all but at-
tached to Angel's right rear tire since we left the house. Hearing Casey's yap, the two deer lurch high into the air and bob
their way over the drifts and out of sight. It looks like fun.

By this time, Mom has caught up, and Angel tells her
about the deer we saw. "*You did?*" she exclaims as Dad revs

---

4. In a recent interview, Mom explained, "I thought it was wrong to
ride fast on Sabbath—or I would have."

his engine and shifts into first. And, as more snow falls gracefully from the clouds, and as Dad, less gracefully, rocks his Honda 175 left and right to make a good trail for his family, I am glad to be on another Sabbath afternoon drive, not fully realizing, yet somehow sensing, that this will be one of my childhood's best memories.

And the thought crosses my mind that some Sabbath afternoon, a few years down the road, it will be *my* turn to make a good trail through the snow for my wife and kids who will love me and who will follow me anywhere—as long as I promise that the way ahead is safe and that we can have hot chocolate with marshmallows as soon as we get back home.

Summer Camp

I never felt the driving urge to go to summer camp that my parents seemed to think I should feel. For one thing, I didn't know anyone at summer camp. Only a couple other kids from my church had gone, and they were never in my age bracket. For another, summer camp didn't offer many things that I couldn't already do. We lived on a lake and had enough yard and water toys to entertain a small nation.[1]

But one cool June evening when I was thirteen, we were sitting on our deck with our neighbors, the Gilberts, and the discussion turned to summer camp and Orlo Gilbert mentioned how he used to "hide in the bushes and kiss the girls" at summer camp, and suddenly the idea gained appeal.

---

1. Some Saturday nights, the church came out and joined us for croquet and whiffleball under the yard lights until we all got hot, at which point we leaped off the dock into the water, where everyone remarked how mushy and gooey the bottom of our lake was, as if it were our fault or something.

"Mom," I said later that evening. "I guess I'll go to summer camp after all."

"Great!" she said. "Do you want to invite a friend along?"

Three Sunday mornings later Mom, Mike Hansen, and I loaded the van and cruised down to Brainerd, home of North Star Camp. Mike had agreed to come along if I would take advanced horseback riding with him. OK, I said, but then he would have to take advanced water skiing with me. OK, he said.

The whole ninety-minute trip I debated whether I should tell Mom to just turn around at the next exit and go back home. Sure, the promises of cute girls and Ski Nautiques sounded nice, but my self-confidence was running low. Peer pressure was for the school year; summer was supposed to be care-free. By the time we pulled into the long dirt driveway where kids with straws in their mouths walked around carrying sticks and being cool, I knew I had made the wrong choice.

"Well, here we are," Mom said cheerfully, and soon we were lugging our bags up to the camp office where they assigned Mike and me to Bear's Den. At least they had kept us together.

"Want me to go to your cabin with you?" Mom asked.

"No, that's OK," I told her. If she was going to abandon me in the middle of nowhere, she might as well do it in one fell swoop.

After unpacking our bags so we could put our clothes in the dresser and then repacking our bags because the dresser was already full, Mike and I walked down to the waterfront where everyone else seemed to be. A boy and a girl were out in a sailboat *all by themselves*. I watched them between pitching horseshoes, which is what we, the loners, did until a friendly blonde boy named Terry walked up and asked us why we weren't wearing swimming bands on our wrists, can't you guys swim?

Of course we could swim. We weren't wearing swimming bands, because *no one had told us* about the swimming test. No one had really told us anything. Apparently, they just assumed that we would figure everything out on our own, our little penalty for not attending North Star all these years.

After barely passing the swimming test, I stood on the shore shivering and toweled off my insecure self while the boy and the girl sailed out even farther. *I'll bet when they go around that bend, he kisses her,* I thought. *In the meantime, I'll just stand here and slide this stupid orange swimming band up and down my wrist.*

"Hey, Andy." It was Mike. "Terry and I are going to go back to the cabin. Meet you there, OK?"

"OK," I said.

This is just great, I thought. *My one friend in this whole place has deserted me, and I'm standing here freezing with an orange band on my wrist and some kid my age is kissing a girl around that bend. Mom was right. North Star Camp is a real blast.*

Back at Bear's Den, things didn't get any brighter. A couple of the guys were planning how we were going to get "honor cabin" for the week. A tall, bony kid named Greg, in a sleeveless shirt, led the discussion. Line call for breakfast is at 7:30, reasoned Greg, so we would need to get up at 5:30 to start cleaning the cabin.

5:30? To do what?

I couldn't believe what I was hearing. Summer camp was quickly turning into boot camp. "All right," said Greg. "Who wants to scrub the shower?"

"You guys are really going to go for it, huh?" said Darrin, our counselor who just walked in. Darrin seemed nice. Plus, he was carrying a wet suit. I went over to talk with him about water skiing, the one thing I felt confident about, and he said that during the winter he skied for Cypress Gardens down in Florida. *Cool*, I thought. Then he said he went barefooting early every morning and that if I ever wanted to go with him—

"Hey, Andy, are you listening?" It was Greg. "You're going to rake the dirt around the cabin, OK?"

"OK," I said.

I raked at 5:35 the next morning, Monday. Then, after breakfast, we had some free time, so Greg told me to rake again. It put me in prime position to see him coming. Curtis.

A towering figure with matted blond hair and big bare feet, Curtis was the boys' director, which meant he inspected all the boys' cabins each morning. By the time he got to Turtle Shell, the next cabin over, I had spread the word and we all stood at attention waiting for him, most impressive if I did say so myself. He didn't even seem to notice us. He dragged his big bare feet through my twice-raked dirt and then scraped them on the ridge of our top step. It bothered me the way he did it. Forty-five seconds later (I timed him) he emerged from our cabin, wrote something on his clipboard, and ambled slowly away.[2]

We didn't make honor cabin on Monday. Terry hadn't tucked in his shoelaces, a half-point deduction. On Tuesday, Greg himself forgot to take out the trash, a whole point. He was too busy telling everyone else what to do that he forgot his own job. By Wednesday, we had pretty much given up hope, so we slept in until 7:00. What was so great about going through the cafe line first anyway?

By Wednesday, I had given up hope in a lot of things. Orlo's remark about the girls had only set me up for a hard fall. The girls didn't even give me a second look,[3] and they never talked about me in private either. I knew this because each evening at campfire, the Nosy Newsers (two girls' counselors dressed up like old ladies) brought us all the latest gossip about who liked whom, and I was never featured.

"Rumor has it," said the first Nosy Newser, "that the girls in Meadowlark Glen cabin have sighted a fox living in Possom Hollow this week. And as it turns out, this fox even has a name: Mike Cox."

"Whoooaaaaaaaaaaaaooo!" everyone went, while Mike

---

2. He would amble away more quickly later that week. I had come back early from horseback riding and he was standing in the woods behind our cabins with one of the girl counselors who was wearing jean shorts over her swimming suit. As soon as they saw me they separated, he going one way, she the other. I noticed that she was pulling up one of her swimming suit straps. It must have fallen down.
3. Maybe it was my striped knee-high tube socks.

Cox's friends patted him on the back and the girls screamed.

"Well, you know," said the second Nosy Newser, "that reminds me of a little saying in Chickadee Hut about another Mike who lives in Possom Hollow: 'There's nobody finer than Mike Wiener.'"

"Whoooaaaaaaaaaaaaooo!" everyone went.

I looked at my friend Mike Hansen, the Mike no girl had noticed. "Boy, I'm sure glad they haven't mentioned my name," I said.

"So am I," he said.

On the way back to the cabin, I wondered how different my life might be if I had been in Possum Hollow with the cool guys. By now, the Nosy Newsers would have included me in their gossip, for sure . . .

"Well, you know," they would have said, "all the girls in this whole camp are saying the same thing: There's no one quite as dandy as Andy."

That's so dumb, I thought. *No girl would say that. Andy's a dumb name, anyway.*

By midweek I knew I wasn't going to meet a girl who wanted to kiss me in the bushes. There weren't any good bushes around anyway. I certainly hadn't seen any flying by on our frantic advanced horseback rides.

Mike had insisted that we take advanced horseback riding because, he said, the other classes would be "boring" and this one wouldn't be. Mike was right—advanced horseback riding was anything but boring, and I thought about how un-boring the class was Monday morning as we galloped *bareback* down a dirt road marred by jagged rocks that would kill a person instantly should a person happen to land on them. *If . . . this . . . class . . . is . . . so . . . advanced,* I thought, pulling my face out from under my horse's throat, *why . . . aren't . . . we . . . using . . . saddles?*

In a week that had taken downturn after downturn, advanced horseback riding was the low point. After peeling me off my horse following Monday's death sprint and then again following Tuesday's show-jumping, my instructor assured me that things were bound to get better the next day. They did.

I hadn't expected to see Dad that week. The only contact I had had with my family was a couple evening phone calls, which were frustrating because the other lonely kids were standing there waiting to use the phone next, are you almost *done?* Mom had eased the pain by sending letters every day stuffed with sports clippings from the *USA Today.* A girl named Mary Lou Retton seemed to be doing well at the Olympics, another thing I was missing.

Wednesday morning, the horse instructor was showing us the different types of horse brushes, not my idea of excitement, when I saw a familiar red Astro van weaving through the woods. *Dad.*

Slipping away from the group, I walked over to where he had parked. I wanted to run. I wanted to swing open the door and hug him. But all the other kids could see us. So I walked.

"Hi, Dad," I said.

"Hi, pal," he said. "Having a good week?"

"Yeah, pretty good," I lied.

"Well," he said, "I was just in the area on business, and I thought I'd swing by and say hello. Do you need anything?"

The question hit me hard. A thick lump filled my throat. Tears tried to fill my eyes, and I had to look at the ground. Yes, I *needed* something. I needed to be with people who thought I was neat. I needed to be home.

"Naw," I said, "I'm all right."

For a moment, no one said anything, but I could feel him looking at me.

"I have an idea," he said. "Why don't you make the most of the next three days, and I'll come early Sabbath morning to get you. Then we'll go home and spend the weekend together, maybe get a volleyball game going Sunday morning. Sound good to you?"

It sounded *very* good.

"Are you sure you don't mind driving down here?" I asked.

"Not at all," he said.

"What about Mike?"

"His mom's coming Sunday morning. Now, do we have a deal?"

We did.

As Dad drove away, something switched in my thinking. Suddenly, it didn't matter so much what everyone thought of me. It didn't matter so much that the girls didn't talk about me in their cabins at night or that the guys didn't think I was cool. It still mattered a little bit, but not as much as it had before. After all, Dad thought I was cool, and Dad was the coolest person anyway.

I took my new attitude with me back to Bear's Den, and remarkably, the tide began to turn.

"Hey, I hear you're a pretty good skier," said a guy from Badger's Burrow in the cafeteria line. I was shocked. Someone had actually noticed me, the invisible camper?

"Oh, thanks," I said.

"Think you could help me get up on one ski?" he asked.

"Sure," I said.

That afternoon I watched from waist-high water as my new friend Chris wobbled, reeled, and lurched his way into the world of slalom skiing. "Whoooohooooo!" he hollered, crossing the wake in a radical crouch. I felt like a proud father.

In the process of helping Chris, I met several of his friends, my favorite of whom was a smiling black kid named Ananda Bates. I had never had a black friend, and I had certainly never seen a guy run as fast as Ananda could. We found a Frisbee and sailed it back and forth in the large grassy area by the flagpole, and no matter how far I threw it, he always caught up.

"Do you want to play pro football someday?" I asked him.

"I sure do," he said. "For the Vikings."[4]

Ananda was my kind of guy. My only regret was that I

4. I made a mental note to never forget the name Ananda Bates in case he ever become a famous football player and I needed Super Bowl tickets. But I've checked the sports page for years, and I've never seen his name.

hadn't gotten to know him sooner. If he had been in my cabin, we probably would have been best friends from the start. But he wasn't from my cabin; he was from Badger's Burrow. I guess I hadn't stopped to think how much someone from Badger's Burrow had to offer.

I was especially disappointed that Ananda and I weren't in the same cabin when they announced Thursday night at campfire that on Friday we wouldn't be going to our regular activities but instead we would be having a camp-wide Olympics. It was the best news I had heard all week. Not only would I *never ever* be forced to ride a horse again, but I would get to experience all the glory and majesty of a full-blown Olympic competition, a significant step up from musical chairs in the church fellowship hall.

Still, a large question loomed: Would Bear's Den even have a chance against such heavyweights as Possom Hollow and Badger's Burrow?

Greg sure seemed to think so. Greg hadn't said much since Tuesday's garbage can fiasco, but with the announcement of Camp Olympics, the old fire began to burn again. Greg barked orders from his corner bunk well into the night, but this time I didn't even resent his self-assumed authority. Planning for the Olympics was important—certainly more important than planning for cabin cleaning—and we needed a heady leader such as Greg.

Twenty-four hours later, we again sat in our bunks, not believing what had happened. The competition had been nail-bitingly close all day. We hadn't gotten any first places, but Greg had taken second to Ananda in the 100 yard dash, and I had surprised everyone (including myself) with second in the hot shot basketball competition. The balls just kept dropping.

"You were unconscious, Andy!" they had said, slapping my back. "Unconscious!"

Unconscious, conscious—I didn't care. I was just glad to help keep my team in the running for a medal. Just doing my part. That's what teamwork was all about—every man doing his part. Still, with all the girls screaming for Possom Hollow, we had no assurance of anything. Perhaps the judges would be influenced by the screams and conveniently slip a few points Possom Hollow's way. "Hey, don't blame us," they would say later, their evil deed exposed by the hungry Brainerd media. "We were just giving the people what they wanted."

After eight grueling hours of competition and several sharp exchanges between hot-headed Adventist kids who hadn't learned how to handle competition, the camp staff assembled us in a giant square around the flagpole. In front of the flagpole stood the awards table, on which lay twenty-four spray-painted wooden "medals"—eight gold, eight silver, eight bronze—each severed by a thick, soft string that would certainly feel most comfortable against the back of my neck.

"OK, people. Let's have your attention."

The camp director was speaking through a megaphone, but not everyone was listening.

"Turtle Shell! Give me twenty push-ups!"

A minute later, after Turtle Shell had hit the deck while

the rest of us laughed, the director continued.

"Now as I was saying, we've had a good Camp Olympics today, and you've behaved yourselves well—with a few exceptions, of course." Everyone laughed again.

"Before we give out the medals," he said, "I'd like to emphasize that winning isn't the important thing. The important thing is that you did your very best and that you had a good time."

Yeah, yeah, I thought. *Let's get down to business.*

"OK," said the director, "at this time we will announce our three winning cabins. If your cabin's name is called, please come forward to receive your medals."

He looked at his clipboard. "The bronze medal goes to Dove's Cove."

The announcement was surprising, but well-received. Warm applause followed the quiet, but athletic girls' cabin as they went forward to receive their medals.

Two left.

"Second place," said the director, "goes to . . . Badger's Burrow."

My heart sunk. I knew that silver was our best hope. Even Darrin, our counselor, looked downcast. *Oh, well*, I thought, as Badger's Burrow trotted to the flagpole. *At least Ananda got a medal.*

"And, finally," said the director, "first place goes to . . ." He paused dramatically. I looked over at the guys from Possom Hollow, some of whom had already taken a step toward the medal stand. *Just get it over with*, I said to myself.

"Beeaaaarrrrr'sssss Deeennnnnnnn!"

The megaphone's echo gave way to silence. Stark silence—except for two sounds: a few soft whimpers from the Possom Hollow women and a wild but concentrated cheer from eight misfits who hadn't had much to cheer about all week. It was a cheer that would be heard many times throughout the rest of the afternoon and evening, diminishing in both intensity and frequency after sundown, but still finding its way up into the quiet night sky of North Star Camp every twenty minutes or so.

"Hey guys, we really did it, didn't we?"

"Yeeaaahhhhhhhhhh!"

It was quiet again as I packed early Sabbath, the day I had so much anticipated. But as I gathered my clothes and flashlight and Bible, I found myself dawdling, pausing every few seconds to reflect on my first week at summer camp. What a change a few days had made. On Wednesday, I would have been packed in about twenty seconds. But the place—and the people—that I'd been so anxious to leave had abruptly claimed a special place in my heart. I panned the cramped cabin. Flip-flops hung from the bedposts, crumpled towels partially blocked the windows. No, we weren't honor cabin material, but we sure could bring home the gold, couldn't we, guys? I looked at my fellow medalists sleeping contentedly—Greg, John, Terry, Mike, and the rest. *Good job, guys. I'll miss all of you.*

I folded my towel around my swimming suit and stuffed them in a side compartment, but as I did, I felt something round and plastic. *What could that be?* I wondered. Then I remembered—the shaving cream! I had forgotten all about it. Last Sunday morning, Dad had sent along six large cans of Gillette Foamy with me—not because I shaved, but because he said they *always* had shaving cream wars at summer camp and I needed to be "prepared."

"Are you sure I need to bring six cans?" I asked.

"You bet," he said. "You're going to need them."

No one had mentioned shaving cream wars all week long, so the cans just sat in my suitcase, which I was now zipping up. On the way out, though, I noticed that the doormat had been kicked off the entry way, leaving a clean four foot by six foot slab of concrete, a canvas just waiting for a message. *Why not?* I said to myself. Shaking up two cans of Gillette Foamy, I knelt on the slab and, in giant white puffy letters, left a reminder for my friends to wake up to: BEAR'S DEN #1. Then, adjusting the gold medal around my neck, I dragged my suitcase to the parking lot where Dad was leaning against the van waiting to bring me home, just as he promised.

Ellen G. White

I met Ellen G. White at a felt board. I was a second grader in a church school classroom; Ellen was a felt school-girl about to be smacked in the head by a felt rock hurled by her felt classmate. As the rock hovered in the air, Mrs. Nash narrated.

"Ellen whirled around just as the rock was thrown. It struck her right in the face."

We clutched our faces and groaned, each trying to outgroan the others. We couldn't imagine the pain. Snow-balls in the face were bad enough. What would a *rock* feel like?

"Did she die?" a girl asked.

"No," replied Mrs. Nash, "but she was sick in bed for a very long time."

The episode lingered in my mind for hours—even through recess. After school, I told it to my friend Michelle Hill who regularly came to my house to play. Michelle wasn't an Adventist, but she was patient, and so she listened as I relayed every detail of Ellen White's childhood tragedy, which we then discussed. The one positive, we decided, about getting hit by a rock was that you wouldn't have to go to school. Still, pain was pain, and we didn't want any part of it.

By the end of the week, I had taken Michelle through Ellen's recovery, the Great Disappointment, and her first vision. "Those who kept their eyes on Jesus stayed on the path," I explained. "But if anyone looked away or tried to show off too much, they fell."

"When they fell, could they get back on?" asked Michelle.

"I don't know," I said. "We haven't gotten there yet."

Ellen G. White's life was exciting to Michelle and me. After all, how many people did we know that could hold an eighteen-pound Bible *straight out* for half an hour, fly with angels while in vision, and describe heaven in detail? Not many. So we had great admiration for this young woman. And we couldn't wait to learn more wonderful things about her . . .

Twelve years later.

I sit reading on a beanbag in a college dorm room. The felts have long since finished, Michelle has moved away, and the word lately is that Ellen G. White isn't so wonderful after all. Again and again, I have listened to church members, classmates, even teachers, ridicule her. It's almost as if they wished that that rock would have taken her out altogether.

For twelve years, I've let others influence my opinion of this "messenger." But now I'm doing something completely radical—checking out Ellen G. White for myself. And, surprise of surprises, thing are getting exciting again.

I'm halfway through the final chapter of *The Desire of Ages*. My heart races as I peek in on the greatest welcome back party in history. Jesus has just risen from the Mount of Olives and is bound for the Kingdom, *His* Kingdom. All heaven is astir as they prepare to escort Him in. The angels are beside themselves. Thirty-three years they have waited for this moment. "They are eager to celebrate His triumph and to glorify their King."

But what's this?

"He waves them back. Not yet; He cannot now receive the coronet of glory and the royal robe. He enters into the presence of His Father. He points to His wounded head, the pierced side, the marred feet; He lifts His hands, bearing the print of nails . . . Now He declares: Father, it is finished. I have done Thy Will, O My God. I have completed the work of redemption. If thy justice is satisfied, 'I will that they also, whom Thou has given Me, be with Me where I am' (John 17:24)."

I'm overwhelmed. The homecoming of homecomings— and all He can think about is His friends on Earth. Those who ditched Him just a few weeks earlier are the ones with whom He wants to spend eternity. And He won't rest until their reservations—until *my* reservations—are confirmed.

"The voice of God is heard proclaiming that justice is satisfied . . . The Father's arms encircle His Son, and the word is given, 'Let all the angels of God worship Him' (Heb. 1:6)." I join them.

On that rainy April evening my freshman year of college, I decided that people could tell me that Ellen G. White wasn't real and that her writings were no longer relevant. That would be fine; let them pitch their pebbles. But they *couldn't* tell me that what stirred in my nineteen-year-old heart as I read a century-old account of Jesus' unfathomable love for this planet—they couldn't tell me that that stirring *wasn't real and wasn't relevant.*

Because it was.

Words

Growing up, most Adventist children will hear upwards of 500 sermons, 300 mission stories, and a couple dozen well-intentioned lectures uttered within the walls of their home church. I was no exception.

While many of these messages, I'm sure, were deeply profound and spiritually nourishing, it isn't the carefully crafted phrase, but the simple expression that claims a permanent spot in my memory . . .

"Well, look who's here!" Years later, I somehow doubt that people like Alice Stutzman, Toby Imler, and Lyle Schmidt built their weeks around the moment I trotted into the church lobby. But they always acted as if they did.

"Good morning . . . good *morning.*" As sure as the word "cordial"[1] and sunset times appearing in the bulletin, the double good morning was an integral part of our church service. The

---

1. As in "We extend a cordial welcome to you . . ." or, for variation, "We cordially welcome you . . ."

reason, of course, for the second "good morning" was that we, the congregation, hadn't responded heartily enough to the initial "good morning." Remarkably, the person who did the double good morning often acted as if he or she was the *first* person to ever think of it. But the double good morning was anything but original. For years—*decades*—the platform speaker had been welcoming people twice. Sometimes, to avoid the second "good morning," I would reply extra-loud to the first. But, as I learned, there was no avoiding the second "good morning." No matter how loud the congregation responds, the speaker will still act disappointed and say it once again: "Good *morning*."

"Praise God from whom all blessings flow." Some weeks, it was the only thing that everyone seemed to agree on.

"And now Andy Nash will bring us our special music." The ten most nerve-racking words in the English language never got any easier to hear. My special music career began with vocal solos (those who currently stand anywhere close to me in church aren't going to believe that) and evolved into saxophone solos. But the anxiety remained at fever pitch.[2]

---

2. The only thing that comes anywhere close to the uneasiness of special music is church roller skating night in Fargo. If you're a boy, you and your buddies race around the rink like madmen for the first half hour. Everyone's in danger. After a while, though, the music slows, the lights dim, and one by one your friends dessert you, skating off with (you can't believe this) *girls*. Somehow, almost by pure fate, no one has yet paired up with your true love who sits drinking orange soda. Unconsciously—as if drawn by a magnetic force—you stumble towards her, a question spinning in your head. As you get closer, though, she looks surprised to see you (she doesn't know she's your true love) and you panic. "Where'd you get that orange soda?" you ask. She tells you and you start to stumble away. But as you go,

From the stage view, the kind, gentle people who had been sitting all around me suddenly seemed angry, impatient, anxious to jump on any mistake I made. Afterward, though, they magically turned nice again—hugging me in the church lobby, heaping on the praise and saying, no, they hadn't even heard that squeak.

"Sorry, altar call is later." It never hurt a pastor to have a sense of humor. One Sabbath, as Pastor Tim neared the conclusion of his sermon, a toddler escaped from the back row and waddled her way down the center aisle toward the pulpit. Realizing that he had lost his audience, Pastor Tim cut short his illustration and gave everyone what they so desperately needed—a chance to laugh.

"Come quickly, Lord Jesus." As a rule, I didn't like long prayers. My knees hurt and my mind wandered. Yet, for some reason, when Jon Aakre prayed long, I didn't keep track. A young dairy farmer, Jon Aakre spoke vulnerably and from his heart. One Sabbath, Jon invited us to kneel with him for closing prayer. In an urgent yet whispered voice, he praised God, thanked God, and then closed with a request: the Second Coming. I *wanted* Jesus to come that day. I wanted to look up and see the roof split like the Red Sea. But as I slowly opened my eyes, everything was normal. The ceiling fan spun. The organ played. The deacons came down to usher us out. Apparently, the time still wasn't right.

---

she says your name and then asks if she can ask you something. You turn around in time to hear her nervous words: "Do you want to skate with me?"

Goodbye

When you attend a small closely-knit church for fifteen-plus years, you don't just pick up and leave. ("Wes, Blanche, it's been real. Have a good life. We're outta here.") How *could* you leave a group of people who have, for all intents and purposes, become family? No, you may not call them Uncle Warren and Aunt Eleanor, as they do down South, but that's what they are—pinch-hitting aunts and uncles, adoring grandparents, fun brothers and boring sisters.

You've been through much with these people the past fifteen years. You've banded together on Sunday mornings, an army of chainsaws, to chop up the Olsons' oak tree, which had quickly lost its majesty as it lay across their driveway. You've welcomed pastors and their families and then, a few years later, watched them drive away, tearful children in the back window. You've plowed each other's driveways a hundred times, jumped each other's cars a hundred more. You've breathed the same air, drunk from the same water fountains, used the same bathrooms. And while the thought of these last few things is enough to make you *want* to move as quickly as possible, you don't. It just doesn't work that way. If you decide to leave, you must leave slowly, dropping hints for at least six months before you make the big announcement.

We left Detroit Lakes in a limited way when I was fifteen and Angel was twelve. (I don't know what Mom and Dad were.) We made the decision for two reasons. First, Dad had a new business opportunity in Florida, something about managing retirement communities—I could never explain it very well.

Second—and more important, they said—was my education. Junior high had taken its toll on my Adventist mind. Plus, a new dimension had entered (complicated) my life: girls. I never admitted it, but they knew —I liked girls now. And in the back of their minds, they were probably thinking about my marrying the right kind of girl someday. I was thinking that I just wanted a girlfriend.

But they weren't ready to ship me off to Maplewood Academy way down in Hutchinson. We were a close family with many good memories yet to make, and we couldn't make these memories with long-distance phone calls. So we decided to take the bare necessities and truck down to Orlando, Florida, for the school year, where Dad could work and I could go to Forest Lake Academy and still live at home, a village kid. Angel would go to the Adventist elementary school. Mom didn't have any definite plans; maybe she would take some graduate classes. So it wasn't a true move. We would be gone for the school year, but then return, conquering heroes, each summer, which was the best time to be in Minnesota anyway—unless you enjoy frostbite.

But it was still a move—our first move of any type—and with it came the expected lumps in throats and tears. Mom led the way. Twelve years of dedicated service (for one-room schoolteachers, there's no other kind) she had given to the Detroit Lakes Seventh-day Adventist Church School. Making lesson plans for eight grades at a time. Playing soccer on whatever team was short a player. Piling the kids into the Subaru every Wednesday afternoon for a trip to the public library—"girls get front seat on the way there, boys on the way back, and I don't want to hear another word about it." She had done it all and then some. She was going to miss it. And they were going to miss her.

We sat in the second row on the right, an unusual place for us, at the Thursday evening 8th Grade Graduation, which this year was doubling as a farewell to Mrs. Nash. For several fifteen-minute intervals, important people got up and said nice things about Mom. We knew it was fifteen minutes because the clock they had bought her as a going-away gift and hid behind the piano was chiming loud and clear every fifteen minutes. Everyone chuckled.

Then Mom got up and, between tears and apologizing for the tears, she talked about how these kids in front of her were her whole life and how she loved every single one of them. I knew that she did. Then she said that, since she was always asking her students to share essays they had written, she thought she would share an essay *she* had written. It was, she said, her favorite memory of the Detroit Lakes church—the day my sister got baptized. She unfolded her essay.

"Other than the miracles of childbirth and rebirth," read Mom, "I do not believe I had ever personally experienced a miracle until the fall of 1985—October to be exact. Many of you were there, but you might not remember the occasion as I do.

"My parents arrived on Friday afternoon, late in October, to attend a very special event for our family. Angel, age 12, after studying the beliefs of the Adventist Church with Pastor Tim, had decided that she wanted to be baptized. We had waited until Grandpa and Grandma Carpenter could come up from Nebraska, and the visit had taken us into a beautiful but cool Minnesota autumn. Even so, Angel wanted to be baptized in our lake—Lake Melissa—where she had swum and played and caught turtles and minnows since she was a little girl.

"We were hoping for a bright, warm-as-possible day. Friday looked doubtful. That evening, in fact, we had the fireplace going and watched as whitecaps formed on the lake and a shrill wind blew. Winter seemed evident and I couldn't bear to think of my little girl going into the freezing water to be baptized. We called Pastor Tim. He phoned the head deacon Lyle Schmidt and told him to fill the baptismal tank for the Sabbath morning service.

"About 9 o'clock Sabbath morning, Tim called with bad news. Lyle had filled the tank, but for some reason the heater hadn't gone on and the water was freezing cold. Pastor Tim wondered whether we should try to go ahead with the lake baptism, which seemed so important to Angel. *Why not?* we decided. In church that morning, it was announced that people would be welcome to come to our place at 4:00 if the weather cleared up. *If.*

"The afternoon, however, got continually worse. At one point, snowflakes fell. Grandma and Grandpa decided that we really should just do it another time and they would understand. After all, we could send them pictures. We tried to call Tim to tell him about the cancellation, but no one was home. So we just sat by the fire and pouted.

"At 3:30 Tim and Becky arrived. There were still white-caps on the lake and a cold wind was blowing. Tim had on a jacket as he came into the house—carrying the baptismal robes, shaking his head. No one expected that there would actually be a baptism that afternoon, but Tim wanted us to know that he wouldn't be making the final decision.

"At 3:45, we sat in the living room, looking out the picture window, and suddenly noticed that the wind seemed to die down. The sun appeared to actually be coming out! Where were the white caps? Where were the snow flurries? We walked outside, and heard some car doors slamming.

"Church people were actually arriving! Many people! The three dozen cookies I had bought weren't going to be enough. We were so touched that our church family—

(At this point, Mom was too choked up to go on. She handed her story to Yvonne McTaggart, who had jumped up to comfort her. Mom seated back beside us, Yvonne continued.)

"We were so touched that our church family would care

enough to travel out for the baptism of one little girl. Especially on such a cold day.

"From that moment through the next hour, I can't remember much, except that we all—family members and friends—gathered out around the lake. Joanne Strom brought her accordion and everyone sang *Alleluia* and *Peace Like a River*. In just a matter of a few minutes, that cold, wintry day turned into a lovely warm afternoon. Everyone took *off* their jackets. It was a miracle!

"No one can ever convince me that the Lord didn't plan that event. Jesus must have said, 'This child is going to be baptized in the lake as she wants; don't spoil My plans!'"

"I have a picture of Pastor Tim and Angel in the still water, sun shining down, autumn leaves showing on the trees in the background. I keep that picture in my Bible and look at it every Sabbath. It reminds me every day that the Lord *is* watching out for my children. He loves them more than I do, if that is possible.

"Twelve-year-old girls usually don't spend their days thinking about the goodness of God or His plans for their life. However, I hope to keep this story in front of Angel so she can know how special she is to the God of the Universe. He turned off the heater in the baptism tank and turned *on* the sunshine at just the right moment. And He can turn other supposedly disappointing times into wondrous surprises! There are miracles all around us, I'm sure, for God *is* a God of love.

"Thank you for listening to my story. We will miss you all."

Apart from some sniffling here and there, the sanctuary

was silent. It was a touching story, a touching thing that the church family had done for us. In fact, I hadn't realized how touched I was until Mom and Yvonne read this story. Suddenly, I was touched to the core. *Moved deeply.*

What a wonderful show of support by our friends! Bundling up and driving out to our lake to watch my sister get baptized. Car doors slamming at a quarter to four. Such nice people. With gratitude, I panned the room. Good old Clarence and Emma. Thank you, thank you both for coming to my sister's baptism. Mildred, Viola, Gladys? Thank you. Thanks—all of you—for what you did. For everything you've done over the years.

When you're fifteen, you only have so many emotions to expend. Mine were expended after two or three minutes, so I made a secret sign to my friends and we went out to our van and got my football. The cool May air felt great as we whipped the ball back and forth in the front lawn; there's something special about playing catch when you're all dressed up. A couple minutes later, Dad emerged from the church lobby and joined us; he had escaped the smalltalk faster than usual.

"Lead me, Dad!" I said, sprinting down the hill, my friends defending on either side. He heaved a tight spiral way up into the sky. I had 'em beat by a step, a sure touchdown, but at the last second Larry stuck out his big hand. The ball spun straight up. Jac slowed down just enough to take out Larry, leaving me in the clear. I snatched the old pigskin out of midair.

"No way!" they said, as I trotted into the lower level

driveway. "You're lucky, Shorts," they said.

I ran back to call a new play, but Mom and Angel were clicking down the sidewalk and we had to quit. Dad and I played catch all the way to the van, our passes becoming shorter and shorter. On the way home, we talked about how we would miss this place *so much* the next winter, but at least we'd get to come back for the summer. One thing was for sure: We would never move away for good.

But, then, we did.

After three years of following the birds south every fall and north every spring, we got the news: Dad's business had collapsed—we could no longer afford such a luxury as a summer cottage. I couldn't believe it. Dad's businesses had always thrived; everything he did succeeded.

We had always had much more than we needed, and Dad always had time to enjoy life with us. But with one announcement, those days were gone. We would sell our cottage and rent a two-bedroom in Orlando. Mom would teach; Dad would find something else to do. We might stay in Florida; we might move somewhere else, like Oregon. But one thing was for sure: We were leaving Minnesota for good.

We spent the summer driving back and forth to the grocery store to get boxes.

Our final Sabbath morning, I stood in the lobby after church and said goodbye to my friends and hugged old people and then went back into the sanctuary to wait for Dad to finish playing the organ. But when I pushed open the door, the organ was silent.

Dad sat in the front row. His face hung in his hands; his shoulders shook. I didn't know how to feel. I had never seen Dad cry before. Reverently, I walked to the front and stood beside him.

"What's wrong, Dad?" I said.

"Oh, nothing," he said, wiping his face. "All set to go, pal?"

"All set," I said.

The next day we auctioned off everything we owned, piece by piece, at an opening bid of five dollars.

The day after that, we drove in to Amoco, filled the tank, checked the hitch one last time, and headed down I-94. It was time to grow up Adventist somewhere else for a while.

From Here

I've been back to visit the Detroit Lakes Seventh-day Adventist Church three times since we moved away for good. There are always a few changes, of course, but the nice thing about small town Minnesota is that nothing changes too quickly. You can be gone several years and come back and walk in the front door and it's like you never left. Helen is still handing out bulletins. Virgil Krogstad is still roaming the lobby, making sure everyone gets greeted. Yvonne is still doing the announcements. Children are still racing up the stairs and shocking themselves on the railing, then shocking each other.

The fall of '94 I made plans to take my girlfriend, Cindy, up to Detroit Lakes so I could show her all the things that hadn't changed and so I could propose to her.

Everything was set. I'd called my friend Jim and asked him to have a small boat tied just off shore of our old place on Lake Melissa on Friday evening so that when I was showing Cindy where I grew up, we could be like *Oh, what's this boat doing here?* and I would say *Well, since it's here, we might as well go for a ride* and I would nobly help her into the boat, and her eyes would start to get big as if she knew something was up, and I would push off shore—never mind that my shoes and jeans got a little wet—and we would glide out onto the soft colors of Lake Melissa, and I would speak from my heart.

I also called the pastor and asked him to put a "Congratulations Andy and Cindy on your engagement" announcement in that week's bulletin, which would really surprise her—*Andy Nash, I can't believe you just assumed that I would say Yes, and what if I had said No? Then what would you have done?*—and I would laugh, and people would say what a creative idea that was, and we would call our friends and relatives and tell them the good news—that Andy had taken Cindy back to his hometown so he could propose to her, and wasn't that romantic?

The night before we were to leave, though, I had to call the pastor and cancel the announcement because on a walk earlier that evening at Andrews University, Cindy told me that, for some reason, she sensed that I was about to ask her to marry me and that even though she *did* want to marry me, she wasn't quite ready to be engaged, so please don't ask yet, OK? So the watch I had picked up that afternoon sat on my closet shelf for another six weeks. She was ready then.

We drove up to Detroit Lakes for the weekend anyway, and I had fun showing Cindy where I had come from. (She had been wondering.) "That's Indian Hill, where we sledded and played the Time of Trouble," I said. "This is the sidewalk where Todd Stutzman used to fry ants with a magnifying glass . . . That's the drinking fountain that I broke moving tables to play floor hockey. See that gash in it? I did that . . . This is the fellowship hall where we had potlucks and church socials."

And as I showed Cindy these landmarks, she would say things like, "Oh yeah, that reminds me of . . ." and, "Oh, I remember doing that." And we would talk about the many childhood memories we had in common.

Memories like "Wink'em." Few things, we agreed, matched the exhilaration, the subtle passion, of Wink'em—how you avoided winking at the person you liked because you were sure that, if you *did* wink at them, they would instantly know that you liked them—how embarrassing!

Or how, if you were already sitting in front of the person you liked and got winked at by someone else, you would wait that extra split-second, long enough to give your true love the chance to grab your shoulders and sit you back down. "Rats!" you would say, slapping your pantlegs, secretly thrilled to spend a few extra moments together.

Cindy could identify with all these emotions and it was fun to reflect on them, even though I wasn't particularly thrilled with the idea of her waiting an extra moment for some Arkansas boy to grab her shoulders, I don't care how long ago it was.

Some of my childhood memories, though, didn't ring any bells with Cindy. "Really?" she would say. "We didn't do that in our church." Or, "Hotdish? What's a hotdish? It's called a casserole. Do you really call it a 'hotdish' up here?" I had never really thought of this before: There was more than one way to grow up Adventist. I had done several things that Cindy hadn't; she might even have done a few things that I hadn't done.

Sure enough, during the next few months, Cindy told me about: being a pastor's kid, being a missionary family in Brazil and Singapore and Texas, attending camp meeting every single summer, going on Pathfinder campouts—things I had not done.

"You've never been in Pathfinders?" she asked. "Oh yeah, it's great. I used to get so envious listening to my sister talk about all the adventures of her Wednesday evenings at Pathfinders making candles, marching, and cooking. I knew my dreams had come true the day that I finally turned ten and got to put on that green dress and yellow scarf and walk to the Pathfinder building. And did I ever walk proudly! Heidi and I took off on our little jaunt, which led us through the academy campus. We heard lots of yelling and whistling and some loud hearty voice from the boy's dorm sarcastically singing, 'Oh we are the Pathfinders strong.' It was so embarrassing!"

Her stories were funny. She could have written a book about them. And so, though we're no longer children, we continue to grow up Adventist together:

waking up Sabbath morning at 8:30, maybe a quarter to nine,

taking our regular spot in church (even getting the giggles once in a while), shaking our heads at the death of a loyal friend, Uncle Dan,

warming up our rollerblades for a Sabbath afternoon drive, chatting on Adventists On-line,

trading in hymns sung *about* God for praise songs sung *to* Him,

discovering the urgent need to reach the unreached,

catching an occasional glimpse of a Saviour looking down, sharing in every joy and every struggle, saying, "Hold on, children—think life is exciting now? Just wait until you see how *decent* life was really meant to be."